DIVERGENT THEOLOGY

AN INQUIRY INTO THE THEOLOGICAL CHARACTERISTICS OF THE WORD OF FAITH, THIRD WAVE MOVEMENT & THE NEW APOSTOLIC REFORMATION

RICHARD P. MOORE

"Richard Moore has done a great service for the church with his inquiry into the teachings of the Word of Faith, Third Wave, and New Apostolic Reformation movements. May many take heed of his warning to consider carefully whether these movements have deviated from theological orthodoxy and to be certain that their zeal for Christ is fueled by truth, not by a spirit of error."

— **Holly Pivec**
Author of *A New Apostolic Reformation?: A Biblical Response to a Worldwide Movement* and blogger at www.spiritoferror.org

"Richard and I have remained friends for over twenty years. He has been a successful youth pastor as well as a devoted husband and father. This is a good book, great for helping believers understand why we are different and how we are similar. I recommend this book, but more so, I recommend Richard Moore, one of the finest men I have ever known."

— **Rev. Michael Holt**
Professor of Youth Ministry 1991-1998, Columbia International University

"Richard Moore's book *Divergent Theology* has opened my eyes more and more to a most serious problem concerning the immediate future of Christian teachings. I am sure his book will be an exposé as well for many among those who are not yet informed concerning the new movements it deals with."

— **Professor Dr. Lothar Käser**
Universität Freiburg, Germany (Retired), Anthropologist/Ethnologist, and Author of *Animismus Einführung in seine begrifflichen Grundlagen (Animism A Cognitive Approach)*

"Richard Moore has discovered something that the entire evangelical church should pay close attention to. This book uncovers a movement that is not easy to detect. It would benefit all church leaders to inform themselves on the theological ramifications so as to shepherd their flocks well."

— **Dr. Andre Rogers**
Professor of Church Ministry, Columbia International University

"Richard Moore has identified and clearly explained a major doctrinal departure from the Bible. He has researched it well and written this important work warning of its effect upon evangelical churches today."

— Dr. Daniel E. Woodhead
President, Scofield Biblical Institute and Author of *The Book of Zechariah: God Remembers Israel's Future*

💬

"Richard Moore masters the difficulty to differentiate delicate theological nuances in postmodern thinking which influences biblical understanding of issues which infiltrate our churches. We need to listen to him in order to avoid wrong developments in theology which have devastating effects on spiritual and biblical understanding."

— Professor Dr. Klaus W. Müller
Freie Theologische Hochschule, Gießen, Germany (Retired), Missiologist and Author of *Das Gewissen in Kultur und Religion (The Conscience in Culture and Religion)*

DEDICATION

This work is dedicated to Ana Katharina Müller Moore,

our daughter who is fearfully and wonderfully made.

I defend the truth of Christ for you

so that people will give glory to God

because of what they see in you.

Divergent Theology: An Inquiry into the Theological Characteristics of The Word of Faith, Third Wave Movement & The New Apostolic Reformation

Copyright © 2017 R. P. Moore

All rights reserved. No part of this publication may be reproduced, stored in a retrieval system, distributed, or transmitted in any form or by any means, including photocopying, recording, or other electronic or mechanical methods, without the prior written permission of the publisher, except in the case of brief quotations embodied in reviews and certain other non-commercial uses permitted by copyright law.

www.richardpmoore.blogspot.com

Cover by https://www.fiverr.com/happy_services

First printing 2017

Scripture quotations are taken from the ESV® Bible (The Holy Bible, English Standard Version®), copyright © 2001 by Crossway, a publishing ministry of Good News Publishers. Used by permission. All rights reserved.

All emphasis in Scripture quotations have been added by the author.

Author photograph and design by www.alltag.li

ISBN-13: 978-1-5404-1603-2

ISBN-10: 1540416038

TABLE OF CONTENTS

Dedication	5
Table of Contents	7
Acknowledgements	8
Introduction	9
Orthodox or Not?	11
What is Divergence?	17
Long Tentacles of Teaching. Theology, and Practice	31
Historical Heresies	37
Gnosticism	41
Gnostic Syncretism Bordering on the Occult	49
Jealous Gnosticism Inside Secrets of the Kingdom	55
Gnosticism Run Amok	59
Christological Heresies: Adoptionism	63
Christological Heresies: Kenosis View	67
Christological & Soteriological Heresies: View of Atonement	71
Christological Heresies: Hypostatic Union	85
Extra-Biblical Revelation	93
Dominionism	103
"Hosting the Presence" or Neo-Gnosticism	111
Danger Within Mainstream Evangelical Christendom	119
The Mysterious Work of the Spirit	123
Indictment of False Teachers and Prophets	133
Conclusion	135
Appendix I: Sources Referenced/Cited	145
Appendix II: Bill Johnson Quotes and Associations	149
Appendix III: Heresies	179
Appendix IV: Scripture References	183
About the author	191

ACKNOWLEDGEMENTS

I would like to thank all the people who have had input on this project. First of all, my wife Simone Müller-Moore, who has encouraged my passion and humility for Christ through this project. I would also like to thank my colleagues at TeachBeyond who have also given me much wisdom into how this work could be accepted into Germany. Benjamin Rudolph, Björn Wagner, and Curtis Coston, thanks very much for your thoughts. I must also thank my parents, Lt Colonel E. Ray and Gail Moore, who have encouraged this work as an important contribution to the evangelical landscape. I would like to thank my father-in-law, Professor Dr. Klaus Müller, for his critical reading and great encouragement to publish and translate this work into German. Thanks also to my sister, Dorothy Moore, who gave many edits and contributions. I also want to thank our church family, Creekside Community Church. Thanks to Pastor John Bruce, and particularly Pastor Jeff Bruce, who gave helpful contributions regarding Christological elements within this book. And finally, this book is written to the glory of Christ. He has given me insight and led me to write this book to warn His Church about a spirit of error.

INTRODUCTION

These are scattered beams; you are the bright sun. These are shallow streams; you are the ocean. These are just shadows, and you are the substance. We are thirsty; we are dry, only you can satisfy. You are the ocean.
—Matt Papa (Contemporary Christian Musician)

Maybe you have had a longing or been thirsty for something more in your Christian life. Maybe you picked this book up with that yearning. Maybe you like me have searched for a deeper more passionate relationship with God. Peradventure you have found what you were longing for in many of the new Christian movements. Perhaps you have heard of some of these new movements, possibly you have never heard of any of these new movements that I will address in this book. This book is for you if you are longing for something more and have searched high and low for something new. This book is also for you if you feel satisfied in your walk with Christ, and don't even know that you are stagnant.

At the very least, my guess is that you have picked this book up probably because you love Christ, His word, and His truth. It is my deepest hope that this book empowers your passion for Him, His truth, and His word. When we hear the truth of God in Christ, it will embolden and empower our zeal for Christ. When our minds are informed about the character and will of God, they will be inflamed with passion for Him. It is, however, possible to have theology in the mind, but for truths not to penetrate our souls. So, it is my prayer and hopeful anticipation that you might let these truths grasp your mind and pierce your soul as you read. The truth must first be understood in our minds before our souls are gripped. In my experience, whenever God's truth pierced my soul, the truth first gripped my mind. My hope is that that you are enthralled by a passion for Christ as you unfold the truth of Theological Orthodoxy (correct or approved doctrines). In unfolding Christian Orthodoxy, it is my hope that you might compare that newly discovered Theology to your current experience in the many modern Christian movements.

If it is your wish to dig deeper or are longing for something more, please stick with me through the rest of this book. I have sought to apply the truth about Christ and the truth of God's word to these new movements that have surfaced in modern Christianity. I want you to explore with me if indeed it is possible for theology to have "swerved" or "diverted" from the truth as Paul talks about in 2nd Timothy 2:17-18. That is where I get the title for this book, *Divergent Theology*. Divergent means differing or deviating. My question is, "Is there such a thing in our day and age as theology that has diverted or differed from Orthodox Theology?" We are all yearning for something more; to obey Christ radically and be touched by something eternal. My hope is that you would be touched, strengthened, or for the first time ever, see the eternal hope that we have in Christ.

I have been deeply touched and strengthened through the research and writing of this project. It has deepened my faith, my love for Christ, and my belief in His power and authority over everything known and unknown to man. And my prayer is that you are also touched again or for the first time with the power, goodness, and saving grace of the one true Savior, Jesus Christ. Come, take this journey with me to find out if there is even such a thing as divergent theology, and how the word of God helps recognize that divergence. As Matt Papa sings in his wonderful song *The Ocean* "These are scattered beams, you are the bright sun. These are shallow streams you are the ocean. These are just shadows, and you are the substance. We are thirsty; we are dry, only you can satisfy. You are the ocean." Everything that we know in this world is a shadow. I hope *Divergent Theology* will help you look to the substance.

ORTHODOX OR NOT?

"I will not glory, even in my orthodoxy, for even that can be a snare if I make a god of it ... Let us rejoice in Him in all His fullness and in Him alone."
—D. Martyn Lloyd-Jones

Like Martyn Lloyd-Jones says, we ought not to glory in orthodoxy because it can easily become an idol, god, or an end in itself. Believing the right things about God cannot alone make us right with God. Jesus has made us right with God on the cross, and that righteousness is applied to us through faith. In the same way, we ought to strive and not let knowledge "puff up" as Paul explains in 1st Corinthians 8:1, "Now concerning food offered to idols: we know that "all of us possess knowledge." This "knowledge" puffs up, but love builds up." The context of Paul's statements is not in relation to theology, but rather the knowledge that foods sacrificed to idols have no real power. But it is not a stretch to apply his statements to all knowledge about God. Therefore, we ought to strive with an attitude of love in our orthodoxy.

What is orthodoxy anyway? The word "orthodoxy" is derived from two Greek words meaning "right" and "honor." Orthodoxy are those doctrines that honor God by characterizing Him correctly. For example, when we build our theologies on the creeds, and statements of the early Church Councils, we can be sure that we have relied on a foundation that has stood the test of time. A rather important part of Christian Orthodoxy is that it claims that it is the only religion to be absolutely true and to provide the only way to God (John 14:6; Acts 4:12; John 3:36; 1 Timothy 2:5). Christian theological orthodoxy represents the message, identity, and mission of the Church throughout the millennia. It is the core of the gospel. It does not vary with the tides of change, the whims of philosophy, or the shifting shadows of time. The timelessness and unchanging nature of orthodoxy is similar to what James says about our eternal God, "with whom there is no variation or shadow due to change (James 1:17 ESV)." The unity of Christian Orthodoxy is not about being right or being wrong. Orthodoxy enables Christians throughout the centuries to have a credible, consistent, and veracious witness to the gospel of the "Lamb of God who takes away the sin of the world."

I chose the cover design of this book for a very specific reason. The tree represents the foundation of Christian Orthodoxy. The birds represent those who have left the shade of that tree, in regards to their errant or divergent theology. In this book, I will deal with a movement that I believe is leaving the shelter of the tree of orthodoxy. That tree of Christian Orthodoxy has given us the perspective and interpretation of the saints from thousands of years of Christian history. It is a solid framework for understanding the teachings of the Bible. Furthermore, it undergirds our faith as Christians. One might have a hard time understanding the gospel if not for our heritage of orthodox underpinnings. I will spend much of my time in this book addressing one particular reason that orthodoxy is so important, specifically that orthodoxy is a safeguard against theological error.

Why is orthodoxy so pertinent and imperative to Christianity? It is because the faith of individual Christians, and the teaching toward that faith is at stake. The diatribe of heresy and orthodoxy has frequently been used to create an atmosphere of intolerance, persecution, or hate. For that reason, many do not like to relate in such terminology and jargon. However, that cannot frighten us away from Orthodox Christianity, because the life and faith of Christianity hangs in the balance. When right doctrines and orthodox teachings are propagated, in a spirit of love, it means that the lives of individual Christians and churches are founded upon the proper fundament, namely the belief and faith in the right savior, Jesus of Nazareth, Lord of all creation.

An indication that Orthodox Christian theology is correct, and not just whim, or fancy, or even the reaction of a few angry theologians at major councils, is that heresy and these improper views of Christ persisted. These same theological heresies appear often in separate ages and totally diverse cultures throughout history. These errors and misrepresentations of the person and work of Christ resurface repeatedly from the early councils until about one thousand six hundred years after Christ. That does not mean however, that they stopped appearing after the Reformation, but rather they continue to resurface in different forms to this day. The reason the faithful councils clearly defined orthodoxy with their creeds and statements is because the message of Christ is the cornerstone to Christianity. Without a proper belief and knowledge of the person and work of Jesus, Christianity is relegated to the status of any other world religion which is based on works (i.e. trying to make ourselves right with God).

Orthodoxy can seem like an insurmountable problem for pastors, theologians and the average Christian. You may ask, why should it affect my everyday life? How does it affect my Christian walk? The fundamental way we live our Christian lives has been based on orthodoxy, whether we know it or not. Theological orthodoxy is not overwhelming. I want to propose rather that it is quite an easy chore. When we re-discover, and refer to the creeds and Ecumenical Councils of antiquity our minds become illuminated and orthodoxy becomes clear. Many assume or argue that Christian Orthodoxy is made up of an oppressively long list of doctrines used to suppress people. However, history confirms that Christian Orthodoxy is most often expressed in magnificent, concise, and beautifully penned short lists of beliefs that describe the Holy Trinity, salvation offered in Jesus Christ, his person, and the meaning of the eternal gospel. The true everlasting gospel of grace is powerful for transformation. On the other hand, the false gospel can and has been used as a weapon of destruction.

Christianity has produced more heresies than any other religion. Why could that be? As previously stated it is the only religion that claims to be completely true. Another reason incorrect heresies arise is that Christianity's truths can be deeply mysterious. Moreover, Christianity has two very strong enemies, the world and the devil. The world and the devil have throughout Christian history sought to influence, and lead the Church away from truth, and especially the truth about Christ, who claims to be the only way to God. If you were the adversary of God what would your tactics be? I would seek to make it very confusing for the average person to understand how to have a relationship with God. If heresies were introduced it might bewilder Christians. As a result of false theologies, our enemy might be able to confuse people on how they can be right with God.

Likewise, the world has also had great influence when it comes to heresies. The ideas and philosophy of man have muddied the waters often in Christian history. The early Christian creeds up to the Chalcedon Creed intended to define clearly the person and work of Christ especially as it referred to errors that had crept into the Church. Now that we have established that Orthodoxy is important, and protects us against error, let us endeavor to align ourselves with the saints of old.

If my children were to walk out into the middle of the street, and I was not to warn them of the danger, then that would not be a loving act. It would rather be an abusive act for me as a parent to let my children play, walk, or get in the way of cars that might cause them real harm. On the other hand, it is a loving act to discipline my children and warn them of imminent dangers as God does with us in His loving discipline.[1] In this heart of love for God, His word, and His church, and to warn the church of impending danger, we can ask if the movements of the Word

---

1 *Heb 12:5-11 (ESV)*

of Faith (WOF), the New Apostolic Reformation (NAR), and the Third Wave Movements (TWM) are actually theologically orthodox or not.

D. Martin Lloyd-Jones points out, we ought to "rejoice in Him in all His fullness and Him alone." During my time working on this book, that has been my constant goal, to rejoice in the Lord. The wonderful part of doing this work is that the research into the true teachings of Christendom have deepened my love for the Lord, and have refreshed my zeal in who He is, and what He continually does for me, the church, and the world. He truly is a perfectly indescribable savior! So, the pursuit of orthodoxy has done wonders for my joy in the Lord and my hope is the same for you that your joy in Jesus would continually abound as a result of reading this book.

Let's take a deeper look at the wider Prosperity Gospel[2] in the process; I believe you will also perceive how wholly unchristian, apostate,[3] and heretical they are. In the coming pages, I will authenticate how the Prosperity Gospel, the Word of Faith (WOF), the New Apostolic Reformation (NAR), and the Third Wave Movements (TWM), do not hold to historically orthodox theologies. In the coming chapters I will cover which historical heresies that these movements teach. Furthermore, this will be corroborated by drawing definitive links to practices that appear to be Occult in nature that this movement engages in. It is my

---

2 *Prosperity Theology is the belief that financial blessing is the will of God for all Christians, and that faith, positive speech, and donations to Christian ministries will increase one's material wealth. This view is based on non-traditional interpretations of the Bible. It sees the Bible as a contract between God and humans: if people have faith in God, He will deliver His promises of security, health, wealth, and prosperity. From these non-traditional interpretations of scripture, they build un-orthodox theologies*

3 *"Apostasy," Wikipedia, accessed April 10, 2016, https://en.wikipedia.org/wiki/Apostasy*

opinion that these movements build un-Orthodox teachings, theology, and practice. The following chapters will further build the argument of how these movements do not embrace true Christian orthodoxy.

CHAPTER SUMMARY

Orthodoxy is the correct and accepted teachings for the Church. It is the adherence to and the agreement with the "Ecumenical Creeds" of the early church.

PROSPERITY THEOLOGY is the belief that financial blessing is the will of God for Christians, and that faith, positive speech, and donations to Christian ministries will increase one's material wealth. This view is based on nontraditional interpretations of the Bible. It views the Bible as a contract between God and man: If man has faith in God, He will deliver His promises of security and prosperity.

WHAT IS DIVERGENCE?

*Jesus is more simple, common, and ordinary than we imagine,
and at the same time the eternal word. He is simple and complex.
He is the true divergence.*

I have noticed a growing trend in Evangelicalism away from the study and knowledge of Scripture, and away from the love of theology of any flavor, not just of conservative theology. I have often wondered where this almost disdain for theology and God's word has come from among Christians. I recently came across one of the classics of Christian literature — *Holiness, its Nature, Hindrances, Difficulties, and Roots* Written by J.C. Ryle. Ryle was an Anglican Bishop of Liverpool in the late 1800s. He had some profound words to say that speaks even to today's Evangelical landscape. He wrote:

There is an amazing ignorance of Scripture among many, and a consequent want of established, solid religion. In no other way can I account for the ease with which people are, like children, "tossed to and fro, and carried about by every wind of doctrine." (Eph. iv. 14.) There is an Athenian love of novelty abroad, and a morbid distaste for anything old and regular, and in the beaten path of our forefathers. Thousands will crowd to hear a new voice and a new doctrine, without considering for a moment whether what they hear is true. - There is an incessant craving after any teaching which is sensational, and exciting, and rousing to the feelings. There is an unhealthy appetite for a sort of spasmodic and hysterical Christianity. The religious life of many is little better than spiritual dram-drinking, and the "meek and quiet spirit" which St. Peter commends is clean forgotten, (1 Peter iii. 4.) Crowds, and crying, and hot rooms, and high-flown singing, and an incessant rousing of the emotions, are the only things which many cares for. Inability to distinguish differences in doctrine is spreading far and wide, and so long as the preacher is "clever" and "earnest," hundreds seem to think it must be all right and call you dreadfully "narrow and uncharitable" if you hint that he is unsound.[4]

Ryle wrote this in 1883, almost one hundred and forty years ago. As I read it, I almost thought he was talking about today. It seems very prophetic and poignant for our time. These words encourage me to write with a single passion to seek to give the Evangelical Church the ability for theological discernment once again, by looking at our roots. When we look at orthodoxy once again, it will center us in truth. We will not so easily be tossed around by every wave of doctrine as Ryle alludes to, but rather we will have a steady anchor, namely Christ and His word.

Cancer is a deadly disease. We all know this. Maybe it has touched you personally or through a family member. We would do anything in our power to rid ourselves of its deadly affects, lest we die. Untreated cancer is not going to heal on its own. You would do everything in your power to get rid of it, including utilizing doctors to help cure you, mainly by getting rid of the cancer to the best of their abilities. Similarly, gangrene is a condition that occurs when body tissue dies. Gangrene cannot be allowed to grow further in a body and must be addressed immediately. Otherwise, the gangrene will spread throughout your bloodstream, and you will eventually die. Gangrene is treated by removing the affected tissue. The cost of removing gangrene is usually the amputation of the affected limb. No one affected by gangrene would dare say, "Well, let's see if it goes away on its own; let's see if it gets better, or maybe this gangrenous infection will improve my health somehow." If you allow the gangrenous condition to con-

---

4 Ryle, J. C., and J. C. Ryle. *Holiness: Its Nature, Hindrances, Difficulties, and Roots: Being a Series of Papers on the Subject.* (London: William Hunt 1883). 9

tinue, you will soon die. The infection will invade your whole bloodstream and poison you from the inside out with its deadening toxins.

These two examples seem like terrible places to be inspired to seek the truth. But I would actually say they are great places to start because no one wants to continue to suffer under either of these illnesses. We would do anything in our power to either stay away from these or to treat them as quickly as possible so as to survive for a long life. Paul, describes in 2nd Timothy 2:16-19, about how false teaching works in the same way. He writes:

> But avoid irreverent babble, for it will lead people into more and more ungodliness, and their talk will spread like *gangrene*. Among them are Hymenaeus and Philetus, who have *swerved* (emphasis added) from the truth, saying that the resurrection has already happened. They are upsetting the faith of some. But God's foundation stands, bearing this seal: "The Lord knows those who are His," and, "Let everyone who names the name of the Lord depart from iniquity."[5]

Paul uses two Greek words in this passage, which make up the basis of my title. The first is γάγγραινα (pronounced gang'-grahee-nah), which is from the root word γραίνω, which means, "to gnaw." Gaggraina (γάγγραινα) can mean ulcer, gangrene, canker, and an eating sore or cancer.[6] This word is only used once in the New Testament, which gives weight to Paul's words and the way in which this "irreverent babble … will spread like gangrene." Paul and the other New Testament writers reserve the harshest language and imagery for false teaching. Here,

---

5 *2 Tim. 2:16-19 (ESV)*

6 *Thomas, Robert L., New American Standard Exhaustive Concordance of the Bible: Including Hebrew-Aramaic and Greek Dictionaries (Holman Bible Publishing, 1981).*

Paul chose a medical term like this, to which his readers would have responded accordingly. The context in which Paul discusses the need to care for false teaching is in his care for Timothy's own theological "workmanship." Paul previously warns Timothy to be on guard with his teaching and ministry and then gives him a prime example of how he can exercise that workmanship by avoiding "irreverent babble." He goes on to describe the poor theological workmanship of two specific people. Hymenaeus and Philetus are the culprits. Peter Williams, in his book, *Opening Up 2 Timothy* describes these two men:

> Here were two heretics who had forfeited God's approval because they were engaged in empty 'godless chatter,' and had undermined the truth of God's Word. Like some *gangrenous* (emphasis added) disease, their false teaching was spreading like a poison, corrupting and infecting the minds and hearts of the people in their understanding of the wholesome gospel.[7]

Furthermore, we see that this gangrene had spread, was continuing to spread, and "destroying the faith of some." That was why Paul addressed Timothy and pleaded with him to "shun profane and vain babblings." Matthew Henry commented on how the spread of these babblings transpired:

> When errors or heresies come into the church, the infecting of one often proves the infecting of many, or the infecting of the same person with one error often proves the infecting of him with many errors.[8]

---

7 Williams, Peter. *Opening up 2 Timothy* (Leominster: Day One Publications, 2007), 58.

8 Henry, Matthew. *Matthew Henry's Commentary on the Whole Bible: Complete and Unabridged in One Volume* (Peabody: Hendrickson, 1994), 2362.

The only solution for these gangrenous heresies, according to Paul, was to shun or avoid them. We would do the same to real cancerous, gangrenous diseases, namely amputation or removal. Paul describes the amputation and removal of Hymenaeus whom he "delivered over to Satan."[9] We could understand this "handing over to Satan" as the shunning, amputation, and elimination of the poisonous heresies that Paul refers to in 2nd Timothy 2.

This brings me to the second word that Paul uses in this passage. It is ἀστοχέω (Pronounced as-tokh-eh'-o). This word is translated here as swerved. This word similarly means to miss the mark, deviate from truth, err, swerve, to be out of line, out of step or cadence with God[10]. It refers to missing God's preferred will by deviating from the counsel of God, and in so doing, stepping outside of His counsel. The word implies the divine disapproval that comes with walking off God's line. It is only used three times in the New Testament, and only in the context of false teaching and false teachers. In this frame of reference, we see that Paul says that these two teachers have developed a theology that diverges from sound teaching, and thus should be met with our disapproval because it is met with divine disapproval. For my purposes, I have summarized the word into one English word: diverge. Divergent means differing or deviating. It is also a mathematical term that means having no finite limits or a sum that is always growing or adding to itself. This is why I have named this book *Divergent Theology*. Paul establishes for us that there are systems of theology and teaching that are against God's will and thus are deviant and divergent. Hence, there is such a thing as false teaching of which God does not approve. So, it follows that we must also watch out for such false teaching. In this book, I address a

---

9   *1 Tim. 1:20 (ESV)*

10 *Henry, Matthew. Matthew Henry's Commentary on the Whole Bible: Complete and Unabridged in One Volume (Peabody: Hendrickson, 1994), 1636.*

divergent theology that deviates from truth. It seems to be continually growing, adding false teaching and practices to itself.

I am not a "Fire & Brimstone" kind of guy. If you knew me, you would know I am a California kid at heart and super laid back, fun loving, and relaxed. I've got to be; I am a youth pastor! So, it is hard for me to start out here, with such a harsh sounding passage of scripture. But when the New Testament writers took divergent theology so seriously, then I must also. That is what leads me to write this book, to seek to protect the Church and the purity of its teaching.

From my research and many years of observation, I have discovered that the *teaching, theology,* and *practice* of the Word of Faith Movement (WOF), Third Wave Movement (TWM), and the New Apostolic Reformation (NAR) are *divergent*. It seems to me that it is gangrenous or cancerous. It may, like Hymenaeus and Philetus, affect much or only a little part of the Body of Christ. As with cancer and gangrene, we cannot allow these deadly infections of our body to exist unopposed, unchallenged, and untreated. We would cause the body to die. Regarding the Church, we might ruin our faith or the faith of those to whom we minister, if we allow the "irreverent babble" to spread in our churches. Let us, like surgeons, remove the deadly infectious teaching of the Prosperity Gospel (WOF), the Third Wave Movement (TWM), and the New Apostolic Reformation (NAR) from our churches.

In this book, I will inquire into the perilous *teaching, theology,* and *practice* of these movements and their leaders, so as to reveal the unsafe nature of the three intertwined movements. Scriptures say we should expose false teachers and *never* take in the poison that they teach.[11] Jesus also instructed us to "beware of false prophets, who come to you in

---

11 *Rom. 16:17-18; 2 Pet. 2:1-3 (ESV)*

sheep's clothing but inwardly are ravenous wolves."[12] These false teachings are often presented as wonderful new movements of God, which is why it's important to expose them. I will show how these movements contain poor theology at best, and at worst, are quite threatening to the greater body of Christ.

As a forewarning, I will spend much time in this book on the teaching and writings of Bill Johnson of Bethel Church in Redding, CA because it affects my ministry in Germany. Likewise, I have personally felt the effects of his teaching when we ministered in California. As I researched his ministry, I have clearly discerned that his influence is extensive, and expansive. Furthermore, I have found his teaching to be most conspicuously divergent. As my research unfolded, I found Johnson was a good cross-section of the teaching and beliefs of the whole New Apostolic Reformation. In fairness to Johnson, he claims to have no connection to the NAR. Nevertheless, I will demonstrate clearly how he has obvious ties to numerous NAR leaders and organizations. Although Johnson claims to have no official connection, he teaches NAR theologies, has unmistakable connections with its leaders, including C. Peter Wagner the father of the NAR. Johnson and Bethel have additionally distanced themselves from mainline Charismatic denominations (Assemblies of God) as other NAR churches have done.

I lived in the San Francisco Bay Area for almost nine years as a youth pastor of a church. There, I was again introduced to the Word of Faith and Third Wave Movements, also known as the New Apostolic Reformation. I had known from my time in Bible College the unbiblical and oftentimes heretical teachings of the Word of Faith Movement. We studied the likes of Robert Tilton, Fred Price, Kenneth Copeland, Kenneth Hagin, Benny Hinn, and Paul Crouch. We studied this move-

---

12   *Matt. 7:15 (ESV)*

ment from a theological and practice perspective why these men were false teachers, how their words and actions taught that God's will for man is that they would be healthy, wealthy, and prosperous, that Jesus suffered the punishment of Satan on the cross (Kenneth Copeland & Kenneth Hagin), and that the Holy Spirit heals with sensationalism (Benny Hinn). Greed and corruption are commonplace in many of these ministries.[13] These ministry leaders use such phrases as "sowing a seed of faith" which is code for giving a financial gift to the ministry in return for the favor of God. Their teaching and movements have been consistently growing inside of contemporary evangelicalism for quite some time. We studied, from their own words, the heretical doctrines they taught.[14]

In my time in California, though, I was reintroduced to what is now being called the "Third Wave Movement" or the "New Apostolic Reformation." From my previous study of the WOF, it became apparent how these newer movements are a development of that same deeply flawed teaching. During our time in California, my wife shared her testimony in a women's Bible study. She shared about our journey with our daughter who has Down Syndrome, and during that particular time, a seizure disorder. My wife during her testimony shared our struggle with Ana

---

13   *"FBI files show televangelist Paul Crouch had suspected ties to ... well, everybody," Muckrock, August 19, 2014, Written by M.G. Lee, Accessed November 3, 2016, https://www.muckrock.com/news/archives/2014/aug/19/fbi-files-reveal-televangelist-paul-crouch-had-tie/ "United States Senate inquiry into the tax-exempt status of religious organizations," Wikepedia, May 6, 2016, Accessed November 4, 2016, https://en.wikipedia.org/wiki/United_States_Senate_inquiry_into_the_taxexempt_status_of_religious_organizations*

14   *Horton, Michael Scott, The Agony of Deceit (Chicago, IL: Moody, 1990) McConnell, D. R., A Different Gospel: A Historical and Biblical Analysis of the Modern Faith Movement (Peabody: Hendrickson, 1988),*

during the time of her devastating seizures. She had something called Infantile Spasms, which is a seizure disorder that only occurs in infancy, and can be very devastating. After sharing her heart in this testimony, a woman approached her and gave her a CD of teaching by Bill Johnson from Bethel Church in Redding, California. The sermon went something like this: "God is good; cancer is bad; Satan is bad; thus, Satan is the source of cancer." While I cannot find that particular sermon in their sermon archives, this is how I remember what he said. He equated cancer with the work of the devil and never a work of, or allowed by God.[15] This would be no surprise if you have any knowledge of the Word of Faith Movement. Bill Johnson was quoted in an interview as saying, "You can only give away what you have. Can God give away sickness? No, He's not sick. You can't give cancer if you don't have it."[16]

This is extraordinarily inaccurate. Of course, God can give away sickness, plague, pestilence, disability, or any other ailment He wishes (see *Christological & Soteriological Heresies: View of Atonement* chapter for explanation of God's sovereignty over healing). He gave leprosy, killed 14,700 people in Korah's rebellion by a plague (Numbers 16), killed Ananias and Sapphira for lying to the Holy Spirit (Acts 5:1–11), He sent instantaneous blindness to Saul (Acts 9:1–9), Elymas the magician (Acts 13:9–12), and the Syrian army that came against Elisha (2 Kings 6:16-22). He struck the firstborn dead when the Angel of the Lord passed over Egypt (Exodus 12). He allowed Job, who was a righteous man, to be struck by boils from the top of his head to the bottom of his

---

15   "Bill Johnson – God is good, ALL the time," YouTube video, 07:31, April 6, 2010, posted by "Whizzpopping," https://www.youtube.com/watch?v=SehJOzfj0Rg, accessed April 10, 2016

16   "Bill Johnson: God Does Not Cause Illness and Never Chooses Not to Heal," Do Not Be Surprised, accessed April 10, 2016, http://www.donotbesurprised.com/2013/08/bill-johnson-god-does-not-cause-illness.html

feet (Job 2). God smote the evil kings of Israel, and even on occasion freed them of their terrible judgements. The Lord struck Jeroboam King of Israel and he died (2 Chronicles 13:20). God struck King Jehoram with an incurable bowel disease. After two years, he became disemboweled because of the disease and he died in agony (2 Chronicles 21:18-19). God did that to Him! God likewise afflicted king Azariah with leprosy until the day he died (2 Chronicles 26:20–21). These are just a few Old and New Testament instances of how God allowed or even pronounced illnesses and occasionally even death. When Johnson says, God can't give away sickness, he is woefully incorrect. One may say that this is the age of grace and God would never behave like this anymore. However, judgement of illness and even death are parsed out like this in the New Testament often. As the word of God says, "For I the Lord do not change; therefore you, O Children of Jacob, are not consumed."[17] And elsewhere it is written, "Jesus Christ is the same yesterday and today and forever."[18]

Johnson also taught in that same interview:

No. Two thousand years ago, Jesus made a purchase. He does not decide not to heal people today. The decision two thousand years ago was to heal. Either the payment was sufficient for all sin or no sin. Either the payment was sufficient for all sickness or no sickness ... The brushstroke of God's redemption was to wipe out the root of sin, the root of illness and the root of poverty.[19]

---

17 *Malachi 3:6 (ESV)*

18 *Hebrews 13:8 (ESV)*

19 *"Bill Johnson: God Does Not Cause Illness and Never Chooses Not to Heal," Do Not Be Surprised, accessed April 10, 2016, http://www.donotbesurprised.com/2013/08/bill-johnson-god-does-not-cause-illness.html*

This did not surprise me, but it did once again bring back into my purview how widespread the Word of Faith Movement had become. Johnson is correct that Jesus sacrifice was truly sufficient for all sins. That must be true; if there was one sin not atoned for, then no sins are atoned for. If there is even one sin for which Jesus did not die, there would be no salvation for anyone. The second cannot be true. Christ's sacrifice was not sufficient for all sickness, because if one sickness is not healed, then He did not die for all sickness. All men die, many from illnesses of one sort or another. Christians still get sick and still die. The Bible nowhere says unambiguously that Jesus died to heal all sickness, it is just not there. If even one single person is not healed, in this line of reasoning, then the atonement is lacking.

People could certainly become discouraged in the Christian life if they don't experience healing for some illness or disability if people held to this teaching. It can cause needless depression and despair. But there is something more at stake than discouragement here. When healing doesn't happen, people might stop seeing themselves as the problem. They might stop thinking that the lack is with them. What I have witnessed happen with individuals involved in these movements, is that they will begin to think that the lack is with the Word of God. That it isn't real or true, and even worse, that Christ's atonement is also insufficient.

This woman's sharing this preaching CD with my wife reminded me that this movement was still there, and it piqued my interest into what the Word of Faith was morphing into: a more troubling, precarious new breed of heresy. As I researched this new movement, I could not believe how deep the rabbit hole went. If one rightly understood the scope of how sin has affected the world and how its ravaging effects completely and thoroughly infect every person,[20] it might better help us in understanding where sickness and death comes from. It comes from Adam; in Adam, all men sinned, and death came through sin.[21] The faithful Christian doctrine through the ages has been that death, disease, and sin are as a result of The Fall, and will not be restored until Jesus returns to make all things fully new. As Millard J. Erickson explains in his seminal work *Christian Theology*,

> We should note that there were other changes as a result of sin. In Eden man had a body, which could not become diseased; after the Fall, there were diseases for him to contract. The curse, involving the coming of death to mankind, also included a whole host of ills, which would lead to death. Paul tells us that someday, this set of conditions will be removed, and the whole creation delivered from this "bondage to decay" (Rom. 8:18-23).[22]

As Erickson explains, we are under a "bondage to decay" until the day when Christ delivers us, and the whole of creation is set free from the bondage of death, disease, and decay. As Christians, we wait with great anticipation.

While I was a youth pastor in California, we had so many people come to us from Bethel in Redding, CA, who were either entirely convinced of the "signs and wonders" that took place there or were total-

---

[20] *Total Depravity is the theological view that was established by Augustine of Hippo and later developed more fully by the Reformers and particularly John Calvin, that says that man is completely and thoroughly affected by sin and cannot respond to God's call of salvation except through Divine Grace.*

[21] *1 Cor. 15:21-23; Rom. 5:12 (ESV)*

[22] *Erickson, Millard, J. Christian Theology, Volume II. (Grand Rapids: Baker Book House, 1984), 613*

ly burned and needed recovery from a false teaching, cult-like atmosphere. This also affected us personally when we received Bill Johnson's teaching CD. It was meant as an encouragement but was received with deep discouragement, and condemnation because our daughter was not healed.

We often had people come from Bethel or WOF backgrounds who asked us if we had faith that God would heal Ana's Down Syndrome. From this teaching, we could have concluded that we did not have enough faith, or that the illness ravaging our daughter's body was from Satan himself. There was no concept of how God might permit and be sovereign over these heinous epileptic episodes for our good and His glory just as the man born blind in John 9 had been born blind, "but that the works of God might be displayed in Him."[23] If I believe that God is sovereign over everything, then He has the power to allow and disallow sickness, as we see in Exodus 4:11, "Who made man mute …" It seemed that only guilt and shame were being delivered by Bethel and the WOF because we could not muster up enough faith for her to be healed of the seizures or Down Syndrome.

Because of my study of these movements, teachings and practices, our personal pain and experiences, and watching others' experiences, I have continued to follow this movement for over fifteen years. If I can help one person to be enlightened and liberated from unbiblical teaching, theology, and practice that I have uncovered, then my purpose has been served. That's my goal in the coming pages.

---

23 John 9:3; Ex. 4:11; 2 Cor. 12:1-10 (ESV)

CHAPTER SUMMARY

Divergent Theology is a theological perspective that has deviated or diverged from God's preferred will or His counsel, and in so doing, has stepped outside of Christian Orthodoxy.

Gangrene is the word that Paul uses to describe two false teachers who were teaching in the New Testament. His admonitions of these false teachers are very strong indeed.

Research will show that the TEACHING, THEOLOGY, and PRACTICE of the Word of Faith (WOF), Third Wave Movement (TWM), and the New Apostolic Reformation (NAR) are divergent.

LONG TENTACLES OF TEACHING, THEOLOGY, AND PRACTICE

"Today, the only heresy is saying that there is heresy."
— *Shai Linne (Christian Hip Hop Artist)*

The tentacles of a false gospel have made their way around the globe. We moved to Germany more than two years ago and had found the Bethel influence is far and wide across Germany. For instance, after preaching recently, a young man approached me and asked to pray that my daughter's Down Syndrome would "go away," because Jesus had paid the price for her health on the cross. I patiently guided this young man into a right teaching of the atonement. I also let him know that it was not a sickness and did not need to be healed. God would not only have to heal her; He would have to change her cellular structure. People with Down Syndrome are born with three chromosomes on the twenty-first strand of every single cell. Down Syndrome is not a disease; it's a chromosomal anomaly. For instance, I love that Ana has the most beautiful walnut-shaped eyes and how the irises of her eyes are speckled! It's amazing. It's who she is. She is "fearfully and wonderfully made."[24] I could not imagine her without Down Syndrome. Could you imagine any of your children without the characteristics that make them who they are? Maybe they have curly hair, black hair, deep blue eyes, silly personalities. People are all shapes and sizes, and those differences make us who we are. I cannot imagine my daughter without one of the most special traits that make her who she is, quirks and all.

---

24 *Ps. 139:14 (ESV)*

Recently, there was an event in Nuremberg, Germany called "Awakening Europe".[25] The speakers were Todd White,[26] Ben Fitzgerald[27] (Bethel Church), and Heidi Baker.[28] This event is put on by God First Ministries and is also endorsed by Bill Johnson, pastor of Bethel Church. I know many people who attended the event in Nuremberg, and many who plan on attending the upcoming events in Freiburg (Stadion-Event) and the rest of Europe. I have experienced many other places and churches using Bill Johnson's sermons and materials from Bethel in Redding. It is hard to find a church that does not use the music put out by Bethel. When Bethel releases a new worship album, it usually is number one on iTunes, the world's largest digital music store, for the first couple of weeks after the album release. This shows the widespread popularity of NAR materials even beyond Evangelical Christendom.

To provide some perspective about the scope and influence of the New Apostolic Reformation, authors Holly Pivec and Douglas Geivett estimate that this movement, which includes the Independently- or Postdenominationally-named segments, could encompass in excess of 369 million worldwide participants.[29] In America alone, they estimate that NAR teaching in some form or another impacts some 66 million

---

25 "Events," GODfest Ministries, accessed April 10, 2016,

http://www.awakeningeurope.com/event

26 "About Todd White," Lifestyle Christianity, accessed April 10, 2016,

http://lifestylechristianity.com/about/about-todd-white

27 "Speakers: Ben Fitzgerald," GODfest Ministries, accessed April 10, 2016,

http://www.awakeningeurope.com/speakers-en/ben-fitzgerald

28 "Speakers: Heidi Baker," GODfest Ministries, accessed April 10, 2016,

http://irismin.org/ and http://www.awakeningeurope.com/speakers-en/heidi-baker

29 Geivett, R. Douglas; Pivec, Holly. A New Apostolic Reformation?: A Biblical Response to a Worldwide Movement. Weaver Book Company. Kindle Edition. (Kindle Location 374).

people.[30] Pivec and Geivett have coined a phrase "Neo-Charismatic" or "Neo-Apostolic" to describe groups that are not necessarily NAR affiliated but often lean toward the NAR vision and teaching. Of those, they estimate 36 million people are directly connected with NAR. Furthermore, they confirmed more specifically through the research of the Center for the Study of Global Christianity at Gordon-Conwell Theological Seminary that 3 million people in America are part of overtly NAR congregations.[31] These numbers show that the movement is obviously burgeoning and its influence is explosive.

The NAR influence is far and wide. Many people I know have had many positive things that they experienced at these events. I do not debate that people have had great and touching experiences. My goal is not to debate those experiences. If you have been involved with any of these events, I sincerely hope and pray that you have experienced Christ in all His fullness. In my opinion, I believe that this movement is not teaching about the Christ that the Bible and Christian history reveals.

I realize these movements are powerful and nothing I write may change what is happening, but if I can help one person think more critically and discerningly about their involvement in these events and teachings, I will have achieved my goal. My desire is to help Evangelicals return to theological discernment.

To give you some background, I want to layout my theology and approach to Scripture. I believe in Full Inerrancy as described in statements such as the 1978 Chicago Statement on Inerrancy. Millard Erickson gives a simple definition of Full Inerrancy:

---

30 *Ibid, (Kindle Location 426)*

31 *Ibid, (Kindle Location 426)*

The Bible, when correctly interpreted in light of the level to which culture and the means of communication had developed at the time it was written, and in view of the purposes for which it was given, is fully truthful in all that it affirms.[32]

To that, we can add 2nd Timothy 3:16–17, which gives us a good basis for understanding and applying Scripture, "All Scripture is breathed out by God and profitable for teaching, for reproof, for correction, and for training in righteousness, that the man of God may be complete, equipped for every good work."[33] For the sake of theological clarity, I have been influenced by the Reformed movement. I hold to all the Church Creeds from antiquity that I will mention later in this book. These theological systems are, however, manmade and in many ways, limited theological systems that have tried to systematize and clarify the Word of God for us. They have succeeded in many ways because these men were brilliant and somehow had a God-given aptitude for creating these theological systems.

These are the views that have influenced me. To read more about my specific beliefs, refer to my blog on that topic.[34]

The following chapters will reflect on the *teaching*, *theology*, and *practice* of the Word of Faith, Third Wave Movements, and the New Apostolic Reformation, mostly from a scriptural point of view. I do this by addressing historically condemned heresies.

---

32 Erickson, Millard, J. *Christian Theology, Volume 1. (Grand Rapids: Baker Book House, 1984), 233-234*

33 *2 Tim. 3:16-17 (ESV)*

34 *Richard Moore Blogspot, accessed April 10, 2016,*
http://richardpmoore.blogspot.de/2015/12/here-i-stand-i-can-do-no-other-so-help.html

I want to be clear that I believe in the supernatural, and that God still acts supernaturally today. I believe in the deep and mysterious work of the Holy Spirit. Cessationism is the view that says that the "sign gifts" ceased with the twelve Apostles and the finalization of the Scriptural Canon. Continuationism is the teaching that the gifts of the Holy Spirit have continued until today, specifically the "sign gifts," such as tongues and prophecy. It is not my goal to debate Cessationism or Continuationism. Both views have good arguments. I try to place myself somewhere in-between the center of biblical tension in regards to these two views of the sign-gifts.

In that tension, I do believe that these gifts should be practiced, in accordance with the Epistles and the New Testament's clear expectations of how these gifts ought to be practiced. There is a clear precedence on how they ought to be practiced in an orderly way, never in chaos, confusion or disarray. I believe that the power of Jesus heals people, and God can use these supernatural acts to build a bridge over a "gospel threshold" (usually in relation to crossing cultural lines). I know many people who have been healed and delivered from crippling illnesses and oppression through the mighty power of Jesus. Our daughter Ana was healed in the end of a crippling seizure disorder.

I have personally, in the powerful name of Jesus, been freed from spiritual oppression and seen His work and power over oppression in my years of ministry, and I have witnessed freedom from oppression in others to whom I have ministered. The story of our daughter is that of healing, but it was not immediate. We prayed often, when healing did not come, we began to pray for grace. God gave it. She has been seizure-free for many years; however, she still has Down Syndrome and we anticipate she will for the rest of her life. This is where I try to stand with brothers and sisters on both sides of the "sign-gifts" camp, all the while seeking biblical integrity. However, it is my opinion, enlightened by Scripture and my years of following these movements that the Word of Faith, Third Wave Movement, and the New Apostolic Reformation are not in the theologically Orthodox Christian camp. In my following arguments, I make every effort to be consistent with historical, biblically-accepted theological assertions along with all the creeds of Christendom.

CHAPTER SUMMARY

The NAR and Bethel Church in Redding, CA have incredible influence far and wide through books, music, conferences, revivals, Christian events, sending Apostles, Prophets, Evangelists, and associates to other places in the world.

The Historic Creeds of Christendom will be our guideposts as to what is theologically orthodox. If a teaching does not line up with the accepted early Christian creeds, then that theology does not fall into the Orthodox Christian camp.

FULL INERRANCY: The Bible, when correctly interpreted in light of the level to which culture and the means of communication had developed at the time it was written, and in view of the purposes for which it was given, is fully truthful in all that it affirms.

CESSATIONISM: is the view that says that the sign-gifts ceased with the twelve Apostles and the finalization of the Scripture Canon.

CONTINUATIONISM: is the teaching that the gifts of the Holy Spirit have continued until today specifically the "sign gifts."

HISTORICAL HERESIES

"The word 'heresy' not only means no longer being wrong; it practically means being clear-headed and courageous. The word 'orthodoxy' not only no longer means being right; it practically means being wrong."
— G.K. Chesterton, "Heretics"

The term heresy is brandished with some degree of ease in our day and age. I would like to define terms that will be used, so as to bring clarity to the subject.

The term "heresy" refers to a false doctrine, i.e. one that is simply not true, and that is, in addition, so important that those who believe it, whom the church calls heretics, must be considered to have abandoned the faith.[35]

Those who I believe have forsaken the faith regarding their documented teachings and quotations I will call false teachers. I will give a breakdown of historical heresies. It is not my intent in this book to look at the positive aspects of the WOF, TWM, and NAR. There certainly may be some positives, like passion for Jesus, passionate worship, excitement in ministry, and enthusiasm, which is appreciated. The greater Church could certainly learn from these.

I want to ask a series of questions to get us thinking about the question of heresy and false teaching. Is there even such a thing as false teachers? And if so, at what point would we say that a false teacher is a false teacher? Would we say he's a false teacher when he teaches that

---

35 Brown, Harold O. J., *Heresies: The Image of Christ in the Mirror of Heresy and Orthodoxy from the Apostles to the Present* (Garden City: Doubleday, 1984), 1

Jesus was not God at some point (e.g. Kenosis Theory)? Would we call him or her a false teacher when they say that there is no Trinity (e.g. Modalism)? Would we call him a false Teacher when he says that the Holy Spirit is also not God but rather a force we could tap into for greater breakthroughs into the supernatural? Would we call someone a false teacher when he employs unbiblical and ostensibly practices that are comparable to the Occult? Would we call someone a false teacher when he says you can earn heaven (e.g. Manifest Sons of God)?[36] Would we call someone a false teacher when he or she makes clear prophetic utterances that turned out to be wrong or inaccurate? Would we call someone a false teacher when they say Jesus will not return until the church is completely unified and the church has dominion of every corner of culture?[37] If a teacher said that there was no resurrection of the dead, would we call him a heretic (this belief is found in Manifest Sons of God theology)? Would we call someone a false teacher that asks his followers to employ Eastern mystic, and New Age practices (soaking, centering prayer, meditation, etc.)? What would it take for us to conclude that a teacher is a false teacher?

---

36 *Manifest sons of God also known as Joel's Army is the teaching that in the last days, a "new breed" of Christians will arise - the "Manifest Sons of God" - who will have supernatural spiritual power and be instrumental in subduing the earth. This view often leads to the belief that the church will not experience rapture (and thus any resurrection of the body) but that the church will move right into total dominion of the earth. And then Christ will return to a unified pure perfect bride. Joel's Army will move in and take over the earth and its cultural spheres (a.k.a. 7 Mountains Mandate)*

37 *Seven Mountains Mandate teaches that, in order for Christ to return to earth, the church must take control of the seven major spheres of influence in society for the glory of Christ. Once the world has been made subject to the kingdom of God, Jesus will return and rule the world. The seven mountains, according to the Seven Mountain Mandate are 1) Education 2) Religion 3) Family 4) Business 5) Government/Military 6) Arts/Entertainment 7) Media*

Unfortunately, all these above-mentioned theologies are taught in some form or other by the NAR.

If the Orthodox teachings of Christendom are not enough for us to label false teachers false teachers, then what is? Do we actually believe the scriptures that in the end times that there will arise more and more false teachers, not less and less? Why do we have such a hard time discerning and calling something heresy when it was clearly labeled heresy in the Bible and historical Christian doctrines? Do we actually believe that there will be teachers as Jesus said, who are like wolves in sheep's clothing? Who is an antichrist and what is the spirit of the antichrist? When the Bible does talk about false teachers in the New Testament, to what or to whom are they referring? And why do Paul and the other New Testament writers save the harshest language for false teachers? It's because doctrine and correct teaching about Jesus are critically important. Some have had their faith ruined, and as a result, have left the faith, or worse yet, a false gospel/practice/faith that is not even near Historical Christendom is allowed to propagate. I tend to think that most Christians would agree that someone who taught the previously stated theologies would be false teachers. At least, that is my hopeful assessment.

These many questions lead me to my purposes which are to point out the poor theology found in the teaching of these leaders and to warn people if they decide to participate. In so doing, my hope is that fewer will be taken in by false teaching and profoundly inadequate and heretical theology. The positives found in these congregations, and the movement as a whole, can be practiced in other congregations. In other words, take those positive aspects, such as passion, and practice them elsewhere.

CHAPTER SUMMARY

The term "heresy" refers to a false doctrine, i.e. one that is simply not true, and that is, in addition, so important that those who believe it, whom the church calls heretics, must be considered to have abandoned the faith.

At what point would we dare to call someone a false teacher? Is there even such a thing as false teachers and heresy? What are we to do about it? We should compare all teachings to Orthodox Creedal Christianity.

GNOSTICISM

Today, take a deep breath; a man rules the universe, Jesus of Nazareth, Son of Mary, Son of God. He ate Fish; He was touchable, and he runs the universe!
— John Piper

(Sermon All Authority in Heaven and Earth, October 8, 2015)

Gnosticism was an offshoot of the early Christian movement that was a blend of self-worship and philosophy. It was the overvaluing of secret knowledge with respect to faith. It has thus been seen as a heretical deviation. Irenaeus was the first to so thoroughly address Gnosticism when he wrote his work *Against Heresies: The Unmasking and Refutation of Falsely So-Called Gnosis*. He wrote it to combat the early heretical influence of Gnosticism into Christendom. Harold Brown defines Gnosticism as:

> The Gnostic position asserts that over and above the simple Gospel, which is all that the ordinary spirits can understand, there is a secret, higher knowledge reserved for an elite. It is natural enough for people to ask more questions than the Gospel answers; the gnostic movement attempted to give the answers, and it did so by drawing on religious sources alien to Christianity and amalgamating them with elements of the Gospel faith.[38]

Gnosticism is particularly devastating to the message of the gospel because it says that there is a "higher knowledge reserved for an elite."

---

38 Brown, Harold O. J., *Heresies: The Image of Christ in the Mirror of Heresy and Orthodoxy from the Apostles to the Present* (Garden City: Doubleday, 1984), 39

This flies in the face of the simple gospel that anyone no matter status in this world can comprehend, receive, and trust the everlasting God through Jesus Christ. The Gospel message and the message of the Scriptures are for all men not an elite class of people who have the ability to uncover its mysteries. Despite the acknowledgment of Gnosticism's heretical history, its ideas of insider secrets continue to this day.

Elements of Gnosticism creep up in many places within the modern Church, but none more prevalent than in the TWM, WOF, and NAR. The elements of Gnosticism are exceptionally strong at Bethel Church in Redding, CA. In a thorough newspaper article from Redding, California, the author Amanda Winters documented the practices of gold dust (a glory cloud filled with gold dust and God's presence) appearing in their meetings, angel feathers (falling from heaven on Bill Johnson and in meetings), and diamonds appearing on people (during intense worship "throne room" sessions).[39] Johnson documents these strange manifestations himself in his book *When Heaven Invades Earth: A Practical Guide to a Life of Miracles*. He claims that small gems have appeared on people, (angel) feathers fall in their church building and other meetings. He says they experience laughter, falling, shaking (in the Spirit i.e. Toronto Blessing), gold dust, oil, and glory clouds as signs of God's presence.[40] Another signal of Gnosticism is found in that same book when Johnson says, "without miracles, there can never be a full revelation of Jesus."[41]

---

39 *"Bethel's 'signs and wonders' include angel feathers, gold dust and diamonds," Record Searchlight, accessed April 10, 2016, http://www.redding.com/news/bethels-signs-and-wonders-include-angel-feathers-gold-dust-and-diamonds-ep-377152155-353401081.html. This article is no longer available on Record Searchlight's website the article can be read here http://www.cerm.info/bible_studies/Apologetics/bethel_church/bethel3.pdf*

40 *Johnson, Bill, When Heaven Invades Earth: A Practical Guide to a Life of Miracles (Shippensburg: Destiny Image Publishers, Inc., 2003) 204-205*

41 *Ibid, 126*

On the next page, Johnson indicates when no miracles are displayed, then there cannot be a complete gospel proclamation.[42]

This teaching destroys the heart of the gospel, which is, that its message may be presented and understood by anyone at any time in any place. The message is the power not any particular miracles, manifestations, or any other insider secret preserved for some elite class of Christian.[43] These practices are wholly unbiblical, and never mentioned in the Scripture but rather mirror a sort of New Age, Eastern Mysticism, or what I would like to label "Neo-Gnosticism" (New Gnosticism). What makes these many practices so devastating is that they have syncretized or combined Pagan practices with Christianity. Christendom has struggled with this and necessitate the need to rid itself of "insider secrets" that Gnosticism purports. These syncretistic streams of Gnosticism were originally condemned as heresy and are creeping back into mainstream Christendom in these new movements. Bethel and others have taken up the practice of syncretizing itself with Pagan, bizarre and other seemingly Occult-like practices. In so doing, they have created a sort of Neo-Gnosticism. They apostate themselves as the Gnostic predecessors have done.

The Neo-Gnostic practices that they label "signs and wonders" such as the "glory cloud" and "gold dust," angel feathers falling, gems appearing, conjuring angel orbs, fire tunnels (in which they employ Kundalini methods),[44] spirit travel, out-of-body experiences, and "healings" are practiced often enough at Bethel that they take great pride in trying to document them. In other words, these strange things have not just happened once. Johnson prides himself that they are a place where

---

42 *Ibid, 127*

43 *Rom 1:16 (ESV)*

44 *"Kundalini," Wikipedia, accessed April 10, 2016,*
https://en.wikipedia.org/wiki/Kundalini

these things regularly happen. They also practice prophecy, portal travel (where people can go through portals to other places physically, so they claim, which is obviously a New Age / Occult practice),[45] extra-biblical revelation, raising the dead, charismatic praying in tongues, soaking, new wine movement, drunken glory, visualization, laughter (Toronto Blessing), and animal sounds while filled with the Spirit. I do not condemn tongues if done orderly as the Bible explains in 1st Corinthians 14:26-40, but the many practices that the NAR employs when "slain in the Spirit" are never mentioned in the Bible.

In relation to the practice of traveling physically to other locations via teleportation or portal travel, the argument arises that things like it happened in the Bible. That is true, but the purpose was not for euphoria, or because of an intense worship time, but rather for the Gospel to travel over cultural thresholds. For example, Philip was commanded by the Holy Spirit to share the Gospel with the Ethiopian eunuch. Directly after the Ethiopian eunuch had been baptized, Philip was "carried away" to Azotus to preach the Gospel further. God wanted the gospel to travel over another particular Gospel threshold. Another occurrence was when Peter had his vision; he was directly thereafter taken to Cornelius' house to preach the Gospel. This vision that Peter had was meant to break him of his view that the Gospel was only for the Jews. There were specific reasons God displayed His power in these ways in the Bible.

These things never happened only for our pleasure or ecstasy, but

---

45 *For the most thorough study of the Occult read and refer to the volume of works by German author Dr. Kurt Koch. His book Occult ABC is one of the best on the subject Koch, Kurt, Occult ABC (Grand Rapids, MI. Kregel Publications 1986). Boa, Kenneth. 2012. Cults, World Religions, and the Occult: What They Teach, How to Respond to Them. (Eugene: Wipf and Stock Publishers). Page 145, 167, 169 (describes Teleportation, and out of body experiences, and Spiritism in communication with the dead)*

rather for the Gospel to travel to those places where it had never before been preached.

Some other NAR practices are contemplative or meditative, where they teach emptying the mind or repeating one word from the Bible, which is not a historical Christian meditative practice. Meditation for the Christian is filling our minds with Scripture. Some of these practices include chanting and soaking, which are taught in Bethel school's SOZO ministry. SOZO is the Greek word translated "saved, healed, and delivered," according to their website.[46]

I remember when soaking, centering, or contemplative prayer sprung out from the Toronto Blessing movement. John and Carol Arnott in around 2005 launched this idea and "certified" other prayer centers worldwide. The NAR has wholeheartedly adopted this practice. And now many NAR churches are steeped in the practice of contemplative, centering, or soaking prayer. These practices have added mystical experiences to the blood of Christ. When we add contemplative prayers, soaking prayers, labyrinths, the "silence," centering prayers, breath prayers, or any other additional work to faith, we demean grace and slip back into a faith built on works. Only the blood of Christ can usher us into the presence of God (Hebrews 10:19).

I have a few observations at this point with soaking or centering prayer. First, soaking/centering is a New Age/Occult-like practice[47] and historically not accepted as a practice in Christendom, but rather has often been rejected for instance within Gnostic mysticism. Second, these practices open people up to all sorts of spiritual powers that could

---

46 "What is SOZO?" Bethel Sozo, accessed October 25, 2016, http://bethelsozo.com

47 Boa, Kenneth. 2012. *Cults, World Religions, and the Occult: What They Teach, How to Respond to Them.* (Eugene: Wipf and Stock Publishers). Page 256

be demonically influenced. Thirdly, there is an order of worship laid out for us in the New Testament that we should adhere to, and soaking prayer, centering prayer or meditative prayer is nowhere to be found in that order of worship. Fourth, meditation is meant to be practiced by faithful Christians, but not the forms of meditation that are taking place in soaking prayer where participants empty themselves and use "sacred words" in mantras, empty their minds, receive healing from His presence, etc. Christian meditation is wholly other. We are commanded to fill our minds with His word, and prayer, and telling God His worth which is worship (Romans 12:1-2). The psalmist showed us how Christian meditation operates when he wrote: " … on His law he meditates day and night."[48]

Additional Neo-Gnosticism is practiced by Bill Johnson's wife, Beni. She uses tuning forks as a prophetic act, and believes she is called to the "prophetic act of waking up angels." She says one of her friends, "gets pretty wacked" when the angels are around."[49] Bill and his wife, Beni Johnson have also contributed to a book called *The Physics of Heaven* by Judy Franklin and Ellyn Davis. Bill wrote two chapters and Beni wrote one. Topics in this book were things such as "The Power of the Zero Point Field" or Dolphin Therapy, "Vibrating in Harmony with God" or healing energy, "Good Vibrations," "Human Sound of Heaven," "The God Vibration," "Angelic Encounters," "Quantum Mysticism," "Mind over Matter," "Sensing Magnetic Fields," and "Human Body Frequencies." Beni Johnson's chapter was the "Clarion Call," in which she describes how the vibrations of Heaven enter into our worship times as Christians. This whole book deals with "exploring the mysteries of God

---

48   *Psalm 1:2 (ESV)*

49   *"Bill Johnson, Jesus Culture and Bethel Church," Shepherd/Guardian, accessed April 10, 2016, https://shepherdguardian.wordpress.com/2013/09/05/heresy-alert-bill-johnson-jesus-culture-and-bethel-church/*

in sound, light, energy, vibrations, and quantum physics." The website for the book even names the contributing authors as "seers."[50]

In a YouTube sermon, Bill Johnson recounted a story where people from his church attended a psychic fair in Northern California. He claimed a woman from his church painted a portrait of three people. She "pressed into it," as he said, and asked the Lord for the names of the people she had painted. She placed the names of the people onto the back of the painting. She then hung them up in their "prophetic booth." People would come into the booth and see themselves painted on the paintings and then the woman who painted the paintings would prophesy over them.[51] This is at best very naïve, and at worst, working in cohort with psychic powers. It appears very similar to those certain psychic Occult practices.[52] I could understand going to a place like this and ministering the Gospel, or praying with people, but to engage in "prophetic" activity that is easily understood as psychic, seer, or medium activity is very dangerous and too near to the practices of those at the psychic fair. In Johnson's story, there was actually no real prophetic value to what happened, just that this woman could see the people and paint a picture of them before she knew them, which sounds more psychic in nature than the biblical gift of prophecy.

Bill and Beni Johnson have also appeared several times on Sid Roth's extremely controversial TV show called "It's Supernatural" where Roth

---

50 *Heaven's Physics, Accessed February 23, 2017, http://heavensphysics.com/*

51 *"Bill Johnson 2015, Revival Alliance Session E," YouTube Video, 2:15:41, a sermon by Bill Johnson on April 6, 2015, posted by SkyLine TV," accessed on April 10, 2016, https://www.youtube.com/watch?v=KdYEzolSHG4&index=4&list=PLCZFj_Ex2zmrGIi8ndK8tpvuNLqP7Iwwm*

52 *Boa, Kenneth. 2012. Cults, World Religions, and the Occult: What They Teach, How to Respond to Them. (Eugene: Wipf and Stock Publishers). 167-169*

has dealt with topics such as angel worship/visitation, portal travel, heaven tourism, eavesdropping on conversations between the Trinity, the Bible Code controversy, teleportation, "downloading the mysteries of money," seeing the invisible spirit world, language/worship of heaven, dream interpretation, and blood moon prophecy.[53] At the very least, this is a lack of discernment on the part of Bill Johnson. But because of the documented patterns of ministry that they exhibit in boundaryless engagement with supernatural realms, it is more likely that he and his wife are in league with Roth and his agenda of accessing the supernatural realm at any cost, whether it is biblical or not.

---

53   "Television," Sid Roth's: It's Supernatural! & Messianic Vision, accessed June 15, 2016, http://sidroth.org/television/tv-archives

CHAPTER SUMMARY

Gnosticism, a heretical deviation, was an offshoot of the Christian movement that was a blend of self-worship and philosophy, the overvaluing of secret knowledge. The NAR has revived Gnosticism. I call it "Neo-Gnosticism." They practice laughter, falling, shaking, prophecy (Psychic Clairvoyance), portal travel, extra-biblical revelation, raising the dead, tongues, soaking or centering prayer, new wine movement, drunken glory, visualization, laughter, animal sounds while Spirit-filled, conjuring angel orbs, fire tunnels, spirit travel or out-of-body experiences, angel worship, heaven tourism, teleportation, dream interpretation, and healings. NAR churches also claim that gold dust, oil, glory clouds, angel feathers, and gems have appeared on people.

GNOSTIC SYNCRETISM BORDERING ON THE OCCULT

"For although there may be so-called gods in heaven or on earth—as indeed there are many "gods" and many "lords"— yet for us there is one God, the Father, from whom are all things and for whom we exist, and one Lord, Jesus Christ, through whom are all things and through whom we exist."
— 1 Corinthians 8:4-6

Syncretism is the mixing and matching of mystical, New Age, or Occult-like practices foreign to that of the Biblical Christian faith with Christianity. Movements can become prey to syncretism when experience becomes more important than orthodoxy. It happens often when missionary movements open themselves up to pagan practices. It is evident from several documentaries and Bethel's YouTube channel how their syncretism and practices that appear to be similar to certain Occult customs work.[54] As seen in the previous chapter, Bill Johnson admits that they practice fire tunnels, gold dust, and have seen angel feathers falling, which he claims have fallen on him and in their meetings for many years. In this clip, he explains in detail what is happening, and he invites more of these manifestations.[55] Johnson claims that God is "intensifying" the manifestations.

---

54 *"Glory Cloud @ Bethel," YouTube video, 03:08, a compilation of the Glory cloud phenomena at Bethel Church in Redding, CA on December 19, 2011, posted by "Bethel.TV Redding," accessed April 10, 2016, https://www.youtube.com/watch?v=lvJMPccZR2Y*

55 *"Response to Glory Cloud at Bethel," YouTube video, 14:17, October 22, 2011, posted by "pastorkimo4960," accessed April 10, 2016,*
https://www.youtube.com/watch?v=tcPkOR4Lwj0

Similarly, many of the early Gnostic movements put a high premium on the ever-intensifying experience of God at the expense of solid biblical teaching or orthodox doctrine. So also, Bethel and Johnson place a high value on experience at the expense of orthodoxy. These are just a few of the practices that Bethel and the NAR employ. Let us have a look now at this teaching that falls under Gnostic syncretism.

Bill Johnson has said that there is a special type of spirituality, a sort of insider intimacy:

> Jesus stood before His disciples, before Nicodemus in John chapter 3, and He made this statement, He said, "No one has ASCENDED into heaven except He that descended" [John 3:13]. Now, this is before His death, before His Resurrection; so He was describing here a lifestyle of intimacy with the Father where even though He was standing on earth, He had ascended into heavenly realms in His relationship with God. The point being, that is an invitation for every believer …[56]

Johnson's Neo-Gnosticism goes several steps deeper when he describes a special spirituality bestowed on the faithful, or as he says, on "obeying the rules of this kingdom."

> Here's what I'm believing for – I know it's never happened, but I know that it must before the end. There must be, not just individuals— I'm thankful we have individuals that are rising up with such anointing, such strength, we have people scattered all over the planet right now that are just making a mess of things in all the right ways. We are so encouraged. But, what I'm believing

---

[56] Johnson, Bill. "Thinking from the Throne." Bethel Podcast. Podcast audio, June 9, 2013. http://podcasts.ibethel.org/en/podcasts/thinking-from-the-throne

for is a generation— a generation that'll rise up with a corporate faith, a corporate anointing to press into realms because it's my conviction that as much as God put on a William Branham, or a Kathryn Kuhlman, or a Wigglesworth, He'll put far greater anointing on a company of people than He ever would on an individual. To do that, there must be that corporate sense of, 'we have to deal with the issue of obeying the rules of this kingdom to tap into the resources of this kingdom' … we cannot use the principles of this world and expect to tap into unlimited resource of the kingdom of God …[57]

In this view, there is a special way to access the unlimited resources of the kingdom of God as Gnosticism has taught since its inception. The danger here is that the Bible makes it clear that anyone can access God through Jesus Christ, our one true mediator, not special anointing or corporate obedience to the rules of His Kingdom. In Christ, we already have everything we need because His Divine power has given us everything we need for living a godly life.[58]

To their credit, Johnson and the NAR camp seem to teach and believe in a great God. Because of that view, I believe they seek to set no limits to His greatness, and particularly how we access Him. From my study of this movement, I think that they believe in a God who is sovereign over every supernatural realm, which is true, and so it follows in their minds; if God is sovereign over every supernatural realm, then He is sovereign over every supernatural practice as well. I believe they desire to "take back" the practices that open those realms up to us. In other

---

57 "The Real Jesus - Part 4 - by Bill Johnson," YouTube video, 14:52, September 2, 2010, posted by "ChasingRiver," accessed April 10, 2016,
https://www.youtube.com/watch?v=vHcRI60j0HI

58 1 John. 2:1; Heb. 12:24; 9:15, 24-28; 5:1-10; 4:14-16; Eph. 2:13; 1 Tim. 2:5; 2 Pet. 1:3 (ESV)

words, I believe they are seeking to recapture the mystical practices that they believe have been usurped from the Church. This is however in contradiction to Biblical Christianity. God, in the Bible strictly forbids practices of the Occult, New Age, and many other mystical practices that are unmistakably off limits for those professing Jesus as Lord.

The Proper biblical view is that God is sovereign and Lord over all supernatural practice and that the gods that have been or currently are worshiped in other religious practices are no gods at all and that the Lord of Heaven's Armies rules them all. Acts 19 is a perfect example of the intersection of the two supernatural forces. In Acts 19, we read that there were believers who had turned to Christ and brought their books of magic and sorcery together and burned them in the sight of all, and the value of the books was thirty thousand pieces of silver. That was probably about $10,000-$20,000 value depending on if it was reflecting the drachma. The result of this book burning was that the word of God grew. This story must have been long remembered in Ephesus. It was proof of honest conviction by the Holy Spirit on the part of the sorcerers and magicians and a remarkable victory of Jesus Christ over the powers of darkness. The work of evil was put to shame. They so rid themselves of these books, so as to never be tempted to return to them again. The sorcerers who came to Christ did not see how they could apply the magic from their books to Christianity, no, they realized that the Word of God is the only law they ought to now live by and that His word and He Himself is sovereign over all supernatural practice. We ought to take heed from this story that shows that we cannot even give any credence to practices that the Bible strictly forbids. I could be mistaken, but in my opinion, these practices dabble too closely with syncretism, and I believe are not Christian in origin.

CHAPTER SUMMARY

Syncretism is the blending of Mystical and or Occult-like practices with Christianity that are foreign to the Christian practice. The Bible Strictly forbids the practices of mysticism, occult, New Age, or anything that falls outside the realm of the worship of the one true God. The NAR and many of its leaders have syncretized strange practices with Christianity. The New converts in Acts 19 are a glowing example of how we ought to act in regard to magic, sorcery and practices that are foreign to Christian worship.

DIVERGENT THEOLOGY

JEALOUS GNOSTICISM: INSIDE SECRETS OF THE KINGDOM

There are no inside secrets to faith. You must not "press in" to something concealed within the kingdom to find it out. You are forgiven in Jesus. He is our mediator before God. By grace through faith, God forgives us because Jesus has been our mediator, is currently our mediator and by faith will continually be our mediator into eternity.

Another teaching that falls into the category of Gnosticism is what Johnson calls "jealously guarding His presence." He teaches that we define the measure of the presence of the Lord that we have access to. On his blog, he writes:

As we become faithful to host the presence of the Lord, we find a tension between two realities—that He has been given to us without measure but that we set the limits of that measure. Though all of the measurements are set up on our end of the equation, we can experience the measure of presence we are willing to jealously guard. Whatever you will jealously guard, that is the measure you will have on a consistent basis. All measurements in the Kingdom exist for us to pursue increase. The whole Kingdom is based on this principle: the faithful use of what you have been given is what qualifies you for more.[59]

---

59   *Johnson, Bill, "Hosting His Presence," January 14, 2013, accessed April 10, 2016,*
http://bjm.org/hosting-his-presence

This jealous guarding of God's presence is the secret formula to receiving more of it. Is this biblical in any form? Absolutely not! God is in control of His glory, presence, and revelation, not any man. As Colossians 3:3-4 says, "For you have died, and your life is hidden with Christ in God. When Christ who is your life appears, then you also will appear with him in glory (ESV)." Jesus is the exact image of the glory of God, and when you have Jesus, you have all the access to the manifold glory of God that you need. There is no secret formula for protecting the glory. God does not need us to protect or jealously guard His glory either, but rather He allows us access to God through Jesus Christ, and only through Jesus Christ is His glory revealed.

Johnson also teaches something he calls a "corporate throne room experience" which he says is necessary to experience more of Jesus than ever before.

> The church will receive a fresh revelation of Jesus, especially through that book ... That revelation will launch the church into a transformation unlike any experienced in a previous age. Why? Because as we see Him, we become like Him! If the revelation of Jesus is the primary focus of the book of Revelation, then we'd also have to admit that worship is the central response. The coming increase in revelation of Jesus will be measurable through new dimensions of worship— corporate throne room experiences.[60]

---

[60] Johnson, Bill, "When Heaven Invades Earth: A Practical Guide to a Life of Miracles (Shippensburg: Destiny Image Publishers, Inc., 2003), 246

The corporate experience is absolutely necessary for us as Christians. The entire New Testament is full of communal Christianity. Nevertheless, we do not need the Christian community to step into His throne room. These "corporate throne room experiences" are in direct contradiction to Hebrews 4:14-16. There we read that every believer through Jesus Christ has direct access to His throne room and that it is a throne of grace and mercy.

> Since then we have a great high priest who has passed through the heavens, Jesus, the Son of God, let us hold fast to our confession. For we do not have a high priest who is unable to sympathize with our weaknesses, but one who in every respect has been tempted as we are, yet without sin. Let us then with confidence draw near to the throne of grace, that we may receive mercy and find grace to help in time of need.[61]

---

61 *Heb. 4:14-16 (ESV)*

CHAPTER SUMMARY

We are allowed access to God through Jesus Christ, and only through Jesus Christ is God's glory revealed (Colossians 2:9; 3:3-4; Hebrews 4:14-16).

"Jealously guarding His presence" Is a NAR teaching that says that we define the measure of the presence of the Lord that we have access to.

DIVERGENT THEOLOGY

GNOSTICISM RUN AMOK

When heresy is found in teaching, it is a dangerous proposition to try to take the good & leave the bad because the roots of heresy will affect the fruit.

The bizarre practices seem not to end, but rather go further and deeper. These strange practices seem to be unhindered, or at the very least, not reined in by these leaders. These strange Neo-Gnostic practices seem rather to be encouraged. Emotions in these movements are whipped up into frenzy. Things have somehow "run amok" in the WOF, TWM, and NAR movement.

Among these many peculiar Gnostic teachings of the "inside secrets of the kingdom," Johnson also practices, with his pastoral staff and associates, something called "grave sucking" (or grabbing). The Youth Apologetics training website describes it as "the belief and practice of pulling the supposed Holy Spirit powers from the dead bones of a previously empowered believer."[62] The aforementioned evangelist, Ben Fitzgerald, Pastor and associate of Bill Johnson and Bethel, who has put on the Stadion-event in Freiburg Germany, among other events in Europe[63] is seen here traveling to the graves of former revivalists and seeking to get the Holy Spirit anointing from their graves.[64]

---

62   Boehm, Michael, "What is Grave-Sucking?" *Youth Apologetics Training (February 13, 2014)*, accessed April 20, 2016, http://youthapologeticstraining.com/grave-sucking

63   "Stadion Event," accessed April 20, 2016, http://www.stadion-freiburg.com/#!programm/cn9a

64   "Bethel Church Soaking up the "anointing" of dead men, or Grave Sucking," YouTube video, 05:44, a description of grave sucking on December 8, 2011, posted by "raider-agent," accessed April 20, 2016, https://www.youtube.com/watch?v=LrHPTs8cLls

If this were the only bizarre thing that these followers of Johnson practiced, it would be enough. In my opinion, this single occurrence would be enough to label him a false teacher. There is no evidence of contrition or renunciation of these practices, but rather deeper and further practice by Johnson and his wife.[65]

Calling up the spirits of the dead is clearly condemned in the Bible. It is called necromancy. It is the conjuring of the spirits of the dead for purposes of magically revealing the future, influencing the course of events, or bringing benefits to the conjurers. Leviticus 19:26; 31, Leviticus 20:6, Deuteronomy 18:10, Galatians 5:19-20, Acts 19:19, 1 John 4:1 and many other Scriptures disallow and strongly condemn this practice. Even the famous act of necromancy that King Saul practiced in 1st Samuel 28 is condemned. Already-dead-Samuel pronounced judgment on Saul for having his spirit called up by the witch of Endor. He rebukes Saul for disobeying the Lord by seeking a medium.

All throughout Scripture, we see that God has condemned this practice as an abomination. Why does God hate this practice? God disallows this because we will put more value on the word (or anointing in this case) of the spirits than the Word of God. Jesus is enough, and His Word is enough. For this reason, it seems to me that, Ben Fitzgerald, who is connected to Bethel and the NAR, is unequivocally a false teacher. If you have thought about being involved in the Stadion-event in Freiburg, Germany, or any other Awakening event scheduled in Europe, use this information to reconsider your involvement. You might be inadvertently affected by these practices and theology.

---

65 *Johnson, Beni, Twitter Post. October 28, 2013, 12:01pm, accessed April 20, 2016, https://twitter.com/prayfor5/status/394901670402228224*

CHAPTER SUMMARY

Necromancy is the conjuring of the spirits of the dead for purposes of magically revealing the future, influencing the course of events, or bringing benefits to the conjurers (the Bible Strictly forbids this practice in Leviticus 19:26; 31, Leviticus 20:6, Deuteronomy 18:10, 1 Samuel 28, Galatians 5:19-20, Acts 19:19, 1 John 4:1).

Leaders and participants of the NAR practice something called "grave sucking" or grabbing. It is the belief and practice of pulling the supposed Holy Spirit powers from the dead bones of a previously empowered believer.

DIVERGENT THEOLOGY

CHRISTOLOGICAL HERESIES: ADOPTIONISM

"Long ago, at many times and in many ways, God spoke to our fathers by the prophets, but in these last days he has spoken to us by His Son, whom he appointed the heir of all things, through whom also he created the world. He is the radiance of the glory of God and the exact imprint of His nature, and He upholds the universe by the word of His power. After making purification for sins, He sat down at the right hand of the Majesty on high,"
— *Hebrews 1:1-3*

Moving on from Gnosticism to the significantly important theologies regarding the nature of Christ. Christology is the study of the nature and work of Christ. The first Christological heresy that I will address is Adoptionism. Adoptionism was a view that "Jesus was born as a mere (non-divine) man, was supremely virtuous and that He was adopted later as 'Son of God' by the descent of the Spirit on him."[66] It is also known as Dynamic Monarchism.[67] Bill Johnson and many other WOF, NAR, and TWM teachers believe and teach this view. Bill Johnson said, "He was born through Mary the first time and through the Resurrection the second time. He was 'born again."[68] In a sermon in 2009, he is quoted as saying, "Did you know that Jesus was born again? I asked … the first service and they said, 'No.' But I will show it. It's in

---

66 *"List of Christian Heresies," Wikepedia, accessed April 20, 2016,*
https://en.wikipedia.org/wiki/List_of_Christian_heresies

67 *Kelly, J. N. D., Early Christian Doctrines (New York: Harper, 1959), 115f*

68 *"Bill Johnson False Teacher," YouTube video, 04:54, two audios from Bill Johnson of Bethel Church in Redding, CA on August 19, 2010, posted by "raideragent," accessed April 20, 2016, https://www.youtube.com/watch?v=UzAwFYKe3h0*

the Bible. He had to be. He became sin."[69] Johnson has also written in his influential book, *When Heaven Invades Earth*, "Jesus laid aside his divinity ... the anointing Jesus received at his baptism was the equipment necessary to make it possible for Jesus to live beyond human limitations."[70] Earlier in that same book, he writes:

> Jesus Christ said of Himself, 'The Son can do nothing.' In the Greek language, that word nothing has a unique meaning—it means NOTHING, just like it does in English! He had NO supernatural capabilities whatsoever! ... He performed miracles, wonders, and signs, as a man in right relationship to God ... not as God.[71]

Johnson further recorded Christological errors regarding Adoptionism when he wrote in his book *The Supernatural Power of a Transformed Mind*:

> Jesus had no ability to heal the sick. He couldn't cast out devils, and He had no ability to raise the dead. He said of Himself in John 5:19, "the Son can do nothing of Himself." He had set aside His divinity ... He put self-imposed restrictions on Himself to show us that we could do it too. Jesus so emptied Himself that He was incapable of doing what was required of Him by the Father – without the Father's help.[72]

---

[69] Ibid., 03:40

[70] Johnson, Bill, *When Heaven Invades Earth: A Practical Guide to a Life of Miracles* (Shippensburg: Treasure House, 2003), 79

[71] Ibid, 29

[72] Johnson, Bill, *The Supernatural Power of a Transformed Mind: Access to a Life of Miracles* (Shippensburg: Destiny Image Publishing, Inc., 2005), 50

Johnson, with these statements, has flirted too closely with Adoptionism, which is extremely dangerous because it denies Jesus divinity. The Son has always been God, never stopped being God while on earth, and will never cease to be God into eternity. To say anything else is to deny the most fundamental Christian doctrine of the pre-existent and eternal Son. The burden of proof is on Johnson to clarify these statements and affirm that he believes that Jesus is from eternity to eternity – the Divine Son of God and did not lay aside His divinity at His incarnation. I have searched to see if he has retracted these quotes. To my knowledge, he has not recanted any of these statements. It appears that he truly believes that Jesus laid aside His divinity. From my readings and copious amount of sermon and online material, it seems that he truly believes that Jesus, for a time on earth, was somehow not God.

CHAPTER SUMMARY

Adoptionism is the view that Jesus was born as a mere (non-divine) man, was supremely virtuous and that He was adopted later as 'Son of God' by the descent of the Spirit on him. It is also known as Dynamic Monarchism.

Bill Johnson and many other NAR leaders teach that Jesus was "Born Again" through His resurrection. Johnson also teaches that Jesus laid aside His divinity.

DIVERGENT THEOLOGY

CHRISTOLOGICAL HERESIES: KENOSIS VIEW

Doctrine, or what you believe, is more important than having an awesome vision, or even great Christian experiences because you will act more on what you believe than what you can envision.

If Johnson's Adoptionism views were not bad enough, Johnson goes on to have an improper view of several other historically-theologically orthodox positions of the Kenosis and Jesus' divinity. Arianism was an early heresy propagated by Arius in the 2nd and 3rd centuries. Arius was declared a heretic at the first Council of Nicaea. Arius taught that the divinity of Jesus Christ took various forms. He taught specifically that the Father created Jesus Christ, that He had a beginning in time, and that the title "Son of God" was a courtesy one.[73] This is unmistakably against the orthodox view of that of the pre-existent Christ.

Johnson wrote in his book *When Heaven Invades Earth*, "He (Jesus) performed miracles, wonders, and signs, as a man in right relationship to God ... not as God. If He performed miracles because He was God, then they would be unattainable for us."[74] This does not mean that Bill Johnson and other WOF, NAR, or TWM teachers are Arians. But this quote and other teachings within this movement are very close to Arianism. At the very least, he and his associates teach Jesus was somehow not God or pre-existent, which is the Orthodox Christian view.

---

73 Kelly, J. N. D., *Early Christian Doctrines* (New York: Harper, 1959), 227f.

74 Johnson, Bill, *When Heaven Invades Earth: A Practical Guide to a Life of Miracles* (Shippensburg: Treasure House, 2003), 29

In the same vein, Johnson and other Bethel Pastors and associates teach a perilous view called the Kenosis. The word Kenosis is derived from the Greek word κενόω, which is pronounced ken-o'-o which means to make empty (figuratively), to abase, neutralize, falsify, make of none effect, of no reputation, void, be in vain.[75] This is used in relation to what Jesus did in the incarnation in Philippians 2:7. He made Himself of "no reputation," "made Himself nothing," or "emptied Himself." What Paul the Apostle is really getting at in Philippians 2:7 is that Jesus gave up His divine rights, privileges, or prerogatives, but never His divinity itself. The widely accepted view is that Jesus emptied Himself of His claims as God, of which He had sole rights to. He did this as an example of how we can live humbly in this life. Colossians 1:15-20 further elaborates on who Christ was as fully God and fully man in one glorious person—Jesus Christ. Colossians 1:19 says, "For in Him all the fullness of God was pleased to dwell."[76] Kenneth Copeland, one of the WOF predecessors to the NAR, is known to have taught the view of Kenosis that Jesus emptied Himself of His divinity while here on earth as an example of how we can be in right relationship with God. Copeland says:

> Christians mistakenly believe that Jesus was able to work wonders, to perform miracles, and to live above sin because He had divine power that we don't have. Thus, they've never really aspired to live like He lived. They don't realize that when Jesus came to earth, He voluntarily gave up that advantage, living His life here not as God, but as a man. He had no innate supernatural powers.

---

75   Thomas, Robert L., *New American Standard Exhaustive Concordance of the Bible: Including Hebrew-Aramaic and Greek Dictionaries* (Holman Bible Pub, 1981)

76   *Col. 1:15-20 (ESV)*

He had no ability to perform miracles until after he was anointed by the Holy Spirit as recorded in Luke 3:22. He ministered as a man anointed by the Holy Spirit.[77]

Johnson and NAR Apostles and Prophets intensify the views of their WOF predecessors like Copeland. As previously cited, Johnson reveals a Kenosis teaching in his book *When Heaven Invades Earth*. Johnson wrote, "He (Jesus) performed miracles, wonders, and signs, as a man in right relationship to God ... not as God. If He performed miracles because He was God, then they would be unattainable for us."[78] It might be understandable if, in the heat of an emotional sermon, Johnson said something like this and was somehow understood out of context, said something he did not mean, or misspoke, but this isn't the case. This was not in a sermon. He wrote it in a book. It was edited and then published as such. And not just in one place in his book, but in several other places, he has clearly said Jesus is/was not God, and has confirmed this WOF profoundly flawed Kenosis view of Jesus.

---

77 Horton, Michael Scott, *The Agony of Deceit* (Chicago, IL: Moody, 1990), 266

78 Johnson, Bill, *When Heaven Invades Earth: A Practical Guide to a Life of Miracles* (Shippensburg: Treasure House, 2003), 29

CHAPTER SUMMARY

Arianism teaches that the divinity of Jesus Christ took various forms. Arius taught specifically that the Father created Jesus Christ, that He had a beginning in time, and that the title "Son of God" was a courtesy one.

Kenosis Theology teaches that Jesus emptied himself of His divinity while here on earth as an example of how we can be in right relationship with God (Kenneth Copeland and WOF teachers).

Bill Johnson and other NAR TWM and WOF teachers teach that Jesus was NOT God or that Jesus laid aside His divinity. They believe that if Jesus had done His miracles as God, then they would be unattainable for us.

CHRISTOLOGICAL & SOTERIOLOGICAL HERESIES: VIEW OF ATONEMENT

"There is more in the atonement by way of merit than there is in all human sin by way of demerit."
— C.H. Spurgeon, "All of Grace"

"The death of Christ is the wisdom of God by which the love of God saves sinners from the wrath of God, and all the while upholds and demonstrates the righteousness of God."
— John Piper

Soteriology is the study of salvation, and all the issues and doctrines surrounding it. One of the many facets of soteriology is the Atonement. There are many different theories and views of what happened in the atonement of Christ and His death for mankind on the cross: the Socinian Theory (the atonement as an example), The Moral Influence Theory (the atonement as a demonstration of God's love), The Governmental Theory (the atonement as a demonstration of divine justice), The Ransom Theory (the atonement as victory over the forces of sin and evil), and finally, The Satisfaction Theory (the atonement as compensation to the Father.)[79]

I adhere to the view of Penal Substitution in light of copious biblical evidence that Jesus death was for us a penal or legal substitute for our sins. Romans 3:21-26 gives us a great deal when it explains the idea of "propitiation." Romans 5:9 is the only New Testament passage that I know of that comes close to saying Jesus' death satisfied the wrath of

---

[79] Erickson, Millard J., *Christian Theology* (Grand Rapids: Baker Book House, 1998), 783-800

God. In addition, these other passages give us a clear picture that the wrath of God will not fall on us because of what Jesus accomplished on the cross. Romans 8:3; 1 John 4:10; Ephesians 5:2; Hebrews 2:17; Hebrews 9:26; 1 John 2:2; and 2 Corinthians 5:21 all fill out the details of Penal substitution and what kind of wrath or punishment Christ might have endured on the cross.

If Jesus experienced the truly weighty wrath of God, it was not because God the Father was angry with God the Son. He was only ever pleased with Him, "This is my beloved Son with whom I am well pleased."[80] He could never be angry or dissatisfied with the Son. God was rather the exact opposite. The Father was so completely satisfied with Jesus' sacrifice for sins that He is graciously able to overlook and expiate ours! They were working together with God the Holy Spirit to rid those who would trust Him by faith of the scourge of sin. The Old Testament sacrificial system is a vastly meaningful reference point for penal substitution. The Book of Hebrews binds Jesus' death and the sacrificial system together. "Indeed, under the law almost everything is purified with blood, and without the shedding of blood there is no forgiveness of sins."[81] The Old Testament system establishes clearly that we need a sin substitute. I can hardly imagine the full wrath of God landing on Christ, however, through the word propitiation, we can know that the "wrath of God was satisfied;" so goes the modern hymn:

---

80   *Matthew 3:17; Matthew 17:5; 2 Peter 1:17; Luke 3:22 (ESV)*

81   *Hebrews 9:22 (ESV)*

In Christ alone, who took on flesh, Fullness of God in helpless babe, This gift of love and righteousness. Scorned by the ones He came to save. 'Til on that cross as Jesus died. The wrath of God was satisfied. For every sin on Him was laid. Here in the death of Christ I live.[82]

Furthermore, Penal Substitution is clearly seen in two major texts: Isaiah 53 which clearly shows that Jesus had the weight of our iniquity upon Him, and 2nd Corinthians 5:21 which says, "For our sake he made him to be sin who knew no sin, so that in him we might become the righteousness of God (ESV)." The whole sacrificial system in the Old Testament explained that man needs a sin substitute (i.e. Penal Substitute). It is also written, "Without the shedding of blood there is no forgiveness of sins."[83] In Christ, God provided that perfect sin substitute. As John the Baptist declared, "Behold, the Lamb of God who takes away the sin of the world."[84]

However, the other Atonement views have worthwhile elements and truths. I also want to clarify that the atonement is deeper, wider, and vaster than we could ever fully know or comprehend.[85] However, Scripture reveals enough for us to know the deep and full details that are sufficient for our understanding. I also want to be generous if others adhere to views besides Penal Substitution. It is my opinion, however, that there are views of the atonement that are wholly unbiblical, and the WOF, NAR, and TWM teach these various unbiblical views.

---

82 *Keith Getty and Stuart Townend, "In Christ Alone," In Christ Alone, Getty Music Label, 2006, copyright by Getty and Townend 2001, Kingsway Music Thankyou Music*

83 *Heb. 9:22 (ESV)*

84 *John 1:29 (ESV)*

85 *Richard Moore Blogspot, accessed April 20, 2016, http://richardpmoore.blogspot.de/2016/02/gospelology-what-is-gospel-thorough.html*

The view that the WOF movement has held for many years is that Christ accomplished our physical healing with His death and that our healing is as primary an act as the forgiveness of sins. Kenneth Hagin, who was undoubtedly influenced by E.W. Kenyon who was a Christian Scientist, first espoused this view. Hagin is often considered the father of the WOF movement and is recognized throughout the movement as a teacher and prophet.[86] McConnell in his book, *A Different Gospel: A Historical and Biblical Analysis of the Modern Faith Movement* clearly established lines from the WOF movement to Christian Scientists and Unity School of Christianity through E.W. Kenyon and Kenneth Hagin. Word of Faith Theology, and particularly the view of the atonement, have been marred by this influence. With that in mind, let us look at the specifics of what has, and is being taught in the WOF movement regarding the atonement.

WOF teaches that Jesus had to die spiritually on the cross. He went to hell to suffer for our sins and was then born-again in hell.[87] If that is not shocking enough – that the eternal God in Jesus Christ had to die spiritually, it gets crazier. Hagin wrote in his book *The Name of Jesus*, "Spiritual death means something more than separation from God. Spiritual death also means having Satan's nature."[88]

Hagin elaborates on the development of this outrageous view on the atonement later on in that same book: "We need to know that healing for our physical bodies is part and parcel of the Gospel of the Lord Jesus Christ. He not only took our sins; He also took our infirmities and bore

---

[86] McConnell, D. R., *A Different Gospel: A Historical and Biblical Analysis of the Modern Faith Movement (Peabody: Hendrickson, 1988),* 55

[87] Hanegraaff, Hank, *Christianity in Crisis (Eugene: Harvest House, 1993),* 153

[88] Hagin, Kenneth E., *The Name of Jesus (Tulsa: K. Hagin Ministries, 1979),* 31

our sickness."[89] The WOF movement was started in the imagination of Christian Scientist E.W. Kenyon, who imparted it to Hagin, who then delivered it as the father of the fledgling WOF movement.

It is hard to find much on the Bethel Church website regarding the cross and their atonement view. To be fair, they do have a little excerpt regarding salvation: "Salvation frees us from the power of the devil — sin, lies, sickness and torment."[90] However, the cross and how to attain that salvation is woefully omitted from this whole page. Especially noticeable in this statement of faith is their silence around wrath, judgment, repentance, atonement, or reconciliation. That omission is even more worrisome than all of the outward heteropraxy (false or unchristian practices). Essentially, the governing center of Bethel's framework is Pentecost, not Calvary. I would posit that any statement of faith that omits the cross is terrifying.

Upon further review, one statement can be found about the cross on another Bethel website, which has more to do with their external international ministry. Buried deep in this website is a fuller statement of faith. "He was crucified for our sins, died, was buried, resurrected and ascended into heaven, and is now alive today in the presence of God the Father and in His people. He is 'true God' and 'true man.'"[91] This statement that is buried a little deeper on this other website, further talks about restoration into fellowship with God. Although this Bethel website does regard the cross of Jesus in this singular occurrence as the means of salvation, it is evident that Pentecost and the supernatural are central to life and ministry at Bethel. It is fairly obvious that the cross

---

89   *Ibid., 122*

90   *"Our Mission," Bethel Redding, accessed April 20, 2016, http://www.bethelredding.com/about/our-mission*

91   *"Who We Are," Bethel, accessed April 20, 2016, https://www.bethel.com/about*

is woefully ignored in Gospel proclamation by Bethel, their Associates, Pastors, Prophets, Apostles, and the greater NAR. I could be mistaken, but it seems to me that Bethel and Johnson have been influenced in their view of the atonement by Hagin and the forerunners of the WOF movement.

The development from the early inception of the WOF view of the atonement has been faithfully handed down to the next generation of Tel-Evangelists, Prophets, and Apostles from Hagin to what we see currently in the WOF, TWM, and NAR. There has been some progression in this theology, but the core of the purpose of Christ's atonement has remained undoubtedly as much about physical healing as the forgiveness of sins. It is clear that the TWM has picked up where the WOF left off. Not only were your sins paid for as Christ suffered the punishment of Satan in hell, but because He had not sinned, God got him out of Hell on a technicality. As God infused the resurrection power back into the spirit of Jesus, He overcame all your sickness, pain, suffering, and, in the meantime, even secured your financial success! Bill Johnson and Bethel echo this terribly inexplicable theological view of the atonement:

> No, two thousand years ago Jesus made a purchase. He does not decide not to heal people today. The decision two thousand years ago was to heal. Either the payment was sufficient for all sin or no sin. Either the payment was sufficient for all sickness or no sickness ... The brushstrokes of God's redemption was to wipe out the root of sin, the root of illness and the root of poverty.[92]

---

[92] "Bill Johnson - Does God Ever Cause Sickness?" YouTube video, 05:02, on October 26, 2009, posted by "Whizzpopping," accessed April 20, 2016, https://www.youtube.com/watch?v=0iXrX9eSHWA

If this was not erroneous and implausible enough, it gets worse. The deficiency of God not healing is not on God's end but rather on our end. Bill Johnson writes on his blog:

> How can God choose not to heal someone when He already purchased their healing? Was His blood enough for all sin, or just certain sins? Were the stripes He bore only for certain illnesses, or certain seasons of time? When He bore stripes in His body, He made a payment for our miracle. He already decided to heal. You can't decide not to buy something after you've already bought it. There are no deficiencies on His end — neither the covenant is deficient, nor His compassion or promises. All lack is on our end of the equation.[93]

Healing is up to God, not up to us. Healing is the sovereign prerogative of God. Many healings that we would have thought should have taken place in the Bible do not. 2nd Corinthians 12:1-10 describes Paul's thorn in the flesh. Most commentators believe it was some problem with his eyes. Job was physically afflicted by the devil at God's permission. Timothy had "frequent illness." Jesus did not heal everyone (Mark 6:1-6). One thing Jesus never did was to produce a miracle without faith (Mark 6:2-3), and He did not produce a "sign from heaven" upon request (Mark 8:11-13), or a miracle that contradicted God's plan (Mark 15:29-32).

Other examples of God's sovereignty are the Apostles. They were killed ruthelessly. In other words, God did not deliver them from suffering and death, but rather at his sovereign command, He permitted their suffering under His gracious hand. Jesus gave us a command to invite

---

93 *"Q&A," Bill Johnson Bethel Sites, accessed April 20, 2016,*
http://bjm.org/qa/is-it-always-gods-will-to-heal-someone

those suffering under the weight of disease and disability into our homes for feasts, but doesn't command us in that same passage to heal those we invite. His hope in the command is rather that we show kindness, and hospitality to those who are suffering (Luke 14:12-14). God, speaking to Moses, displays his ultimate sovereignty over illness and disability, "Then the Lord said to him, "Who has made man's mouth? Who makes him mute, or deaf, or seeing, or blind? Is it not I, the Lord?""[94]

Another example, Mephibosheth, the son of Jonathan, in the Old Testament was injured in an accident and crippled. David took it upon himself after Jonathan's death to show kindness to the house of Jonathan and invited Mephibosheth into his home to eat at his table for the rest of his life (2 Samuel 4 & 9). Leviticus displays to us that taking care of the disabled, and those who are suffering, has something to do with our reverence for God, "You shall not curse the deaf or put a stumbling block before the blind, but you shall fear your God: I am the Lord."[95] In other words, if there is no reverence for God then one might not care for those suffering under disabilites. If, on the other hand, there is a fear and reverence for the Lord, then there will be a care for people who are suffering under these disabilities. Healing, suffering, and diseases are more about God and his sovereign plan than about our hope for immediate healing.

God, in the Old Testament, often weilded sickness, ailments, disease, disability, even plagues to His sovereign ends. The rebellion of Korah in the Old Testament is a prime example. God killed with a plague 14,700 people in one day as a judgement on rebellion (Numbers 16). God often used these circumstances as judgement on people for wickedness. However, He also allowed these situations for His glory, for instance,

---

94 *Exodus 4:11 (ESV)*

95 *Leviticus 19:14 (ESV)*

Naaman in the Old Testament. It says that the Lord had given victory to Syria because of Naaman and he was a mighty man of valor. He had the favor of God, but he also had leprosy. Naaman sought healing from Elisha, and God gave healing, inasmuch as He had allowed the leprosy to begin with. John 9 is the most stunning instance of God's sovereignty over disability and illness. The Disciples see a man born blind and ask Jesus "Rabbi, who sinned, this man or his parents, that he was born blind?" Jesus responds to them, "It was not that this man sinned, or his parents, but that the works of God might be displayed in him."[96] God had allowed the blindness in this man that he would one day encounter Jesus, and the works of God would be put on display in and through him.

Additionally, those born with disabilities are woven together in their mother's womb by the all powerful hand of a good and loving God. Psalm 139 describes a God who "knitted me together in my mother's womb." Everyone, everywhere from Adam to the present who has ever been born have been God's wonderful kneedlework. He has formed each and every person uniquely in our own individual ways. In the same vein Paul describes that the body of Christ needs weaker members. 1st Corinthians 12:12–27 says, "the parts of the body that seem to be weaker are indespensable,"[97] which shows us that we need those who are frail to make the body of Christ whole. Without the weaker parts of the body of Christ the church is not complete. Healing, health, birth, life, death, suffering, sickness, and disease are all given or permitted according to the prerogative of an almighty supreme God, not according to our sufficiency or deficiency.

---

96   *John 9:1-3 (ESV)*

97   *1 Corinthians 12:22 (ESV)*

When and if God chose to heal people it happened, and continues to happen in response to an effectual faith, in accordance with His great mercy and kindness. Johnson would have us believe if people are not healed that the, "lack is on our end of the equation." If Christ purchased our atonement on the cross and our sins past, present, and future are forgiven then our healing ought to have also been accomplished immediately. Just as our full atonement is consummated upon repentance and faith, so also should our healing according to this logic. If we were to apply Johnson's teaching fully, Christians who have placed their faith in Christ, should never get sick. In actuality our full and complete healing will not be achieved until we receive our incorruptable bodies at the resurrecton of the righteous.

The previous quotation from Johnson is to me a crass reminder of my own experiences of the control, the hurt, the pain, the guilt, and shame that this cult-like message from Bethel and Bill Johnson produces. The covenant is not deficient; all lack is on our end of the equation. If we took Johnson's teaching at face value, our daughter is infused with a disease from Satan, and our faith is too weak to secure her healing. The lack is on our end of the equation, and that is why she is not healed. This was so offensive and hurtful to us as a family so many years ago, but our feelings are not the crux of the matter, the truth is. If this were true, as previously stated, then all believers, as soon as they put their trust in Christ, would immediately be free from illness, poverty, and death, because Christ bore our illness and poverty on the cross, just as He did our sins. If our sins are forgiven and are gone, so also should all our sickness, disease, torment, and poverty. In actuality, they are not done away with. The truth is, even the Christian will struggle under these until we receive our glorified bodies and death is finally done away with.[98]

---

98 1 Corinthians 15:12-58 (ESV)

The reality is that we die and death is the ultimate illness. About one-third of people who die daily die of some sort of illness. About two-thirds of daily deaths are people who die naturally of old age (that number is almost 90% in industrialized countries). The only way that Johnson can get away with this disconcerting view is that he qualifies it with the phrase "all lack is on our end of the equation." If we die of cancer as a Christian, the lack must have been on the cancer victim's end. But that is precisely where the perspective breaks down. We all die at some point. Death is the ultimate disease, which takes this perplexing theology out of the realm of the logical and moves it into the realm of the absurd.

This view certainly pours on the guilt, shame, and hurt when God does not heal despite deep faith and hopeful prayers. Surely God can and does heal us when we pray in faith,[99] but does God do it as a rule? Or is it connected to the forgiveness of our sin? Is healing bound up into the atonement of Christ? The other possibility is that of the historic orthodox view of Christianity. In Genesis 3, when sin entered the world, it affected everything. Death entered the world through one man's disobedience as Romans 5:12, 19-21 shows us:

> Therefore, just as sin came into the world through one man, and death through sin, and so death spread to all men because all sinned … For as by the one man's disobedience the many were made sinners, so by the one man's obedience the many will be made righteous. Now the law came in to increase the trespass, but where sin increased, grace abounded all the more, so that, as sin reigned in death, grace also might reign through righteousness leading to eternal life through Jesus Christ our Lord.[100]

---

[99] *James 5:13-16 (ESV)*

[100] *Rom. 5:12, 19-21 (ESV)*

We can see here that the obvious judgment on Adam's race was death and decay, but on the other hand, by the one man's obedience, many will be made righteous. No mention of the restoration of health, wealth, or prosperity, but rather in verse 21 a righteousness leading to eternal life. So yes, one day He will restore our lowly bodies at the resurrection of the righteous,[101] but until that day, the earth is "groaning with the birth pangs."[102]

In conclusion, this view is perilous because it creates an inclusion to the cross of Christ that has not been historically accepted in any of the manifold views of the atonement. The only verse that could be used, as a proof text, is found in Isaiah 53:5, which says, " … and by His wounds we are healed." The danger here is to build a whole theology from one isolated text. Take, for example, the passage in Mark 16:18 that says we will pick up serpents and drink deadly poison and not be hurt. We cannot build a whole theology and practice off one proof text. Unfortunately, many churches do practice snake handling and drinking poison. Did Mark and Isaiah mean that we ought to practice these things? We should rather address the "whole counsel of God" when addressing puzzling passages of Scripture so as to clarify their meanings. The WOF, TWM, and NAR add the element of health, wealth, and prosperity into the atonement that has never before been hypothesized, and in so doing, expand the atonement to unbiblical boundaries.

---

101 *1 Cor. 15:12-49 (ESV)*

102 *Matt. 24:8; Mark 13:8 (ESV)*

CHAPTER SUMMARY

Soteriology is the study of salvation, and all the issues and doctrines surrounding it. There are many different theories and views of what happened in the atonement of Christ and His death for mankind on the cross.

Penal Substitution is the view that Jesus death was for us a penal or legal substitute for our sins.

The atonement is deeper, wider, and vaster than we could ever fully know or comprehend. However, Scripture reveals enough for us to know the depth and width that are sufficient for our understanding.

The WOF, TWM, and NAR add the element of health, wealth, and prosperity into the atonement that has never before been hypothesized, and in so doing, expand the atonement to unbiblical boundaries.

DIVERGENT THEOLOGY

CHRISTOLOGICAL HERESIES: HYPOSTATIC UNION

Jesus' Hypostatic Union, the fact of His two natures in one glorious person, makes Him a reliable prophet, priest, & King!

> *"Jesus was God and man in one person, that God and man might be happy together again."*
> — George Whitfield

The Hypostatic Union is the theological term for the union of the two natures of Christ. In AD 451, the Council of Chalcedon defined the two natures of the hypostasis, which is Greek for "person." The historically-theologically accepted position that the council established is that Christ had two distinct natures: humanity and deity. There is no intermingling of natures, and although He had two natures, He is one person. This position that the Chalcedon Creed established is accepted by all of Christendom, namely all Orthodox, Catholic, and Protestant Christians.[103] The Chalcedon Creed reads,

> Following, then, the holy Fathers, we all unanimously teach that our Lord Jesus Christ is to us One and the same Son, the Self-same Perfect in Godhead, the Self-same Perfect in Manhood; truly God and truly Man; the Self-same of a rational soul and body; co-essential with the Father according to the Godhead, the Self-same co-essential with us according to the Manhood; like us in all things, sin apart; before the ages begotten of the Father as to the Godhead, but in the last days, the Self-same, for us and for our salvation (born) of Mary the Virgin Theotokos as to

---

103 *Driscoll, Mark, and Gerry Breshears, Doctrine: What Christians Should Believe (Wheaton: Crossway, 2010), 230*

the Manhood; One and the Same Christ, Son, Lord, Only-begotten; acknowledged in Two Natures unconfusedly, unchangeably, indivisibly, inseparably; the difference of the Natures being in no way removed because of the Union, but rather the properties of each Nature being preserved, and (both) concurring into One Person and One Hypostasis; not as though He were parted or divided into Two Persons, but One and the Self-same Son and Only-begotten God, Word, Lord, Jesus Christ; even as from the beginning the prophets have taught concerning Him, and as the Lord Jesus Christ Himself hath taught us, and as the Symbol of the Fathers hath handed down to us.[104]

As seen before, it seems that Bill Johnson does not believe in the historical findings of the Council of Chalcedon that reveal that Jesus was one glorious person in two distinct natures. Instead, Johnson has said that Jesus laid aside His divinity and that Jesus was only a man completely dependent on the Father during His time here on earth. The Hypostatic Union is another theological position that Bill Johnson and other NAR teachers, prophets, and apostles deny. Because of this mounting evidence, I have formed the opinion that Johnson is a false teacher. Scripture confirms that anyone who denies that Jesus is the Christ is an antichrist and liar, and if denial of the Son happens, then that person also does not have the Father.[105]

However, if we were to extend generosity to Johnson, we might acknowledge that he is trying to explain the seemingly inexplicable hypostasis. For instance, let us address when Johnson describes Jesus

---

104 Bindley, T. Herbert, and F. W. Green, The Oecumenical Documents of the Faith; the Creed of Nicaea, Three Epistles of Cyril, The Tome of Leo, The Chalcedonian Definition (London: Methuen, 1950), 91-92

105 1 John 2:20-25 (ESV)

laying aside His divinity. If we were very charitable with him on his description, we could conclude he is talking about Jesus rightfully assuming a human nature. It is difficult to understand why Johnson describes Jesus laying aside His divinity at all. That is quite inaccurate. In Christ taking on flesh, He laid aside none of His divinity, just His divine rights. He held His divine prerogatives loosely as a man. Moreover, it is incorrect to say that Christ never operated in this world using his divine privileges, just that he acted with limits. Christendom's theological history has tried to make sense of the nature of Christ by explaining that Jesus's hypostasis did not divinize His humanity (i.e. no intermingling of natures).

Eutyches was an archimandrite in the early 5th century who taught that Jesus had one nature, or that Jesus became one nature.[106] We could conclude from Johnson's teaching that he might be in line with Eutychianism or Monophysitism. Monophysitism, as it became later known, was the greater teaching of Eutyches (Mono=Single, Physis=nature).[107] On the other hand, Contra-Eutychianism was the reaction to Monophysitism and taught that Christ didn't divinize His humanity and that He retained two natures as the aforementioned Chalcedon Creed explains in detail. Johnson could be affirming the orthodox view that Christ legitimately assumed a human nature, but it seems improbable from the context of Johnson's quotes. The context is in relation to being able to do what Jesus did. His point appears to be that if Jesus had retained His divinity here on earth, then we would not be able to do the miraculous things that He did because we can't do what God does. His other statement that Jesus operated here on earth as man, not as God,

---

106 Erickson, Millard J., *Christian Theology* (Grand Rapids: Baker Book House, 1998), 729

107 Ferguson, Sinclair B., David F. Wright, and J. I. Packer, *New Dictionary of Theology* (Downers Grove: InterVarsity, 1988), 442

confirms at the very least that his language is careless or sloppy, and at the very worst, that he really means that Jesus completely laid aside His divinity and operated only as a man on this earth.

These elements of Johnson's teaching could be leaning toward a material heresy rather than a formal heresy. Material heresy is spoken or written teaching, whether on purpose or by accident, which goes against Orthodoxy. It is an opinion that is contrary to the teachings of the Church or broader Christendom. Formal heresy, on the other hand, is proposed by someone deliberately and is consciously teaching against orthodox Christendom. If we were to give Johnson the benefit of the doubt, then one could lean toward understanding His teaching as material heresy.

Christ did have to lay aside certain privileges as God in His human nature, for instance, Jesus's humanity was not everywhere, it didn't know everything, it could be tempted, etc. If we took his statements that way, Jesus was really a human entirely dependent on God, as Johnson seems to be teaching, who did miracles through the power of the Spirit. In other words, Jesus didn't go around pulling out His "God-card." Concessions to his meaning could be made, but his other quotes and teachings about the nature of Christ produce great questions and raise many red flags. They are suspicious and beg to be clarified. The burden for clarity lies with Johnson.

To clarify his Christological comments, I reached out to Bill Johnson, to see if he would like to explain these particular Christological quotes. I was successful in reaching his personal assistant. She replied and asked if I wanted "to know the truth" and if I was "seeking out real answers and responses from us." I replied with these several quotes asking for clarity and if he really stood by those quotes. I have gone back and forth with his assistant several times. Her last correspondence explained, "I do doubt that Pastor Bill will respond, as there is nothing that he would feel the need to recant for. He most fully believes in the full deity of Christ which seems to be your charge of heresy is that he doesn't. This is an error and mistake on your part. As well, we are not a part of NAR, again another error in the book. We have had others who have also printed such errors and then afterward, felt the need to recant and apologize, once they realized the mistake."

If he does believe in the deity of Christ, then the plethora of quotes to the contrary are at least very confusing. Johnson has to have access to theologians who could have helped clarify his published works with more precision but seems as if those quotes were left unclear instead. A teacher who says and writes that Jesus somehow "laid aside His divinity" without precise explanation and exposition is quite irresponsible.

If anyone had even intimated that I was a false teacher, and had taught that Jesus was not God, I would make every effort to correct, explain, or even withdraw my comments that were misunderstood or unclear. I would seek to realign myself with all historical creeds of Christendom, which Johnson easily could have done, and biblically accurate teachings, rather than wander between confusing statements. If I had made comments about Christ that were vague, sloppy, inconsistent, haphazard, or otherwise diminished His person in any way, then I would bend over backward to correct or retract what I had said or written. But rather, it seems like Bill Johnson stands behind all these previous citations.

I am not the only one who has questioned the teaching of Bill Johnson there are a plethora of theologians, pastors, Christian leaders, bloggers, writers, and vloggers that have similarly critiqued his writing and teaching. I reached out to many leading theologians and church leaders in the process of writing this book. The support they gave was overwhelming for what I was doing in analysis of Johnson's teaching. Even though several leaders did not want to give me a recommendation quote for concern about pushback, there was undoubtedly support for what I was doing. That is why I will let those who I contacted remain nameless here. Please understand though that the Evangelical theological landscape is aware and deeply concerned at the developments in the NAR.

In private correspondence, his personal assistant communicates that he believes in Christ's deity, but in public discourse, he asserts a very confusing message of the deity of Christ. He could have easily aligned himself with the creeds that explain the details of Christ's Hypostasis, but he has rather shown an aversion to theology and anything that could be gleaned from it (See Appendix II troubling Bill Johnson quotes). I have in the previous chapters sought to establish that his Christological statements are at least careless in their handling of the nature of Christ, and more than likely exceptionally inaccurate.

His assistant also said in our last correspondence that they "are not part of NAR," however, the associations are clear. He may not have any official organizational connection (there is no official NAR organization, only loose affiliations). He is nevertheless, a part of the revival alliance, which has many NAR leaders within its ranks. He also has appeared at Todd Bentley's commissioning service with the "who's who" of NAR leaders that was broadcast on GOD TV. He later appeared with Rick Joyner in a video to restore Todd Bentley into ministry. He even wrote an update on Todd Bentley published on MorningStar's ministry website.[108] All of his books have endorsements, and forwards from prominent NAR leaders. He also appears often in speaking engage-

---

108   "Update on Todd Bentley-Note From Bill Johnson," Accessed March 7, 2017, MorningStar Ministries Website, https://www.morningstarministries.org/resources/special-bulletins/2011/update-todd-bentley-note-bill-johnson#.WL53NRiZO8U

ments with other NAR leaders. He appeared at events in Germany with Randy Clark, Heidi Baker, Ché Ahn, and John Arnott. Other upcoming International appearances include those with Shawn Bolz, Georgian and Winnie Banov, Patricia King, and Randy Clark, all of which, have NAR ties. He teaches a course at the Wagner Leadership Institute called "Walking in the Supernatural."[109] This school was started by C. Peter Wagner one of the forerunners of the NAR movement.

Furthermore, He has written chapters of books in partnership with other NAR leaders and authors (i.e. *The Physics of Heaven* mentioned earlier). He endorsed *The Passion Translation* of the Bible along with other NAR leaders including Ché Ahn (refer to Extra-Biblical Revelation chapter). He appeared at the Azusa Now event in California with many other NAR Apostles and leaders including Lou Engle (of TheCall). He even appeared in their promotional videos for upcoming events with TheCall.[110] So, the claim that they are not a part of the NAR is not entirely true. Johnson and Bethel may not have an official partnership with the NAR, but it is unmistakably clear that they are aligned deeply with the NAR and its theological background.

---

109 "Walking in the Supernatural," Accessed March 11, 2017, Wagner Leadership Institute Website, http://wagnerleadership.org/course/pw828/

110 "TheCall: The Next Chapter," YouTube Video, 1:20, on December 20, 2016 posted by "thecallvideos," Accessed March 7, 2017, https://www.youtube.com/watch?v=vRjbbdljTdA

CHAPTER SUMMARY

The Hypostatic Union is the theological term for the union of the two natures of Christ. The Council of Chalcedon defined the two natures of Christ's hypostasis. They defined that there is no intermingling of natures, and although He had two natures, He is one person.

Eutychianism or Monophysitism teaches that Jesus had one nature, or took one nature.

Contra-Eutychianism was the reaction to Monophysitism, and taught that Christ didn't divinize His humanity. It teaches that He retained two natures as the Chalcedon Creed explains in detail.

Bill Johnson and other NAR, TWM, and WOF teachers teach a form of Eutychianism that says Jesus was only human or that He became one nature in the person of Jesus. Johnson's Christological teaching probably falls under Material Heresy and not purposeful more serious Formal Heresy.

Material Heresy is spoken or written teaching, whether on purpose or by accident, which goes against Orthodoxy.

Formal Heresy is proposed by someone deliberately and is consciously teaching against orthodox Christendom.

EXTRA-BIBLICAL REVELATION

"I warn everyone who hears the words of the prophecy of this book: if anyone adds to them, God will add to him the plagues described in this book, and if anyone takes away from the words of the book of this prophecy, God will take away his share in the tree of life and in the holy city, which are described in this book."
— *Revelation 22:18-19*

The next danger that permeates the WOF, TWM and NAR is what is called "extra-biblical revelation." Extra-biblical revelation is any information or content outside the Bible either in the form of knowledge or experience which gives us information concerning God, His work or His will, which is not directly from the Bible. It can also be teachings, concepts, and practices that claim to be supported by or taught in the Bible, but which are based on incorrect interpretation. Within hermeneutics (the science of Biblical interpretation), this practice is known as eisegesis. Eisegesis is superimposing a meaning onto a biblical text, as opposed to the proper form of hermeneutics, exegesis, which is drawing the meaning out of the text.

Leaders and participants in these movements are constantly looking for a "word of wisdom," meaning that an apostle, teacher, or evangelist will bring a new word from God. This can be as simple as "God said …" or as complex as creating another teaching that is nowhere to be found in the Bible. An example of this is when Bill Johnson wrote in his book, *The Supernatural Power of a Transformed Mind*, "Revelation is not something you can dig out of a Theological book or study guide. It's not even something you can unravel in the Bible all by yourself."[111] The

---

111 Johnson, Bill, *The Supernatural Power of a Transformed Mind 40-Day Devotional and Personal Journal* (Shippensburg: Destiny Image Publishing Inc., 2011), 1 Introduction

freedom for personal interpretation of the Bible was won for us during the reformation and confirmed by the Church of Jesus ever since. The implication from Johnson is that you can only unravel what the Bible means with Johnson's or another prophet/apostle's help through his words of wisdom, explanations, and books, of which there are plenty.

He might also be trying to communicate that it takes more than just reading the Bible; the Holy Spirit is necessary. Jesus said, "When the Spirit of truth comes, he will guide you into all the truth ... Sanctify them in the truth; your word is truth."[112] It seems to me that Johnson's view takes authority away from the Bible and personal interpretation. How will God, in the end, speak to man? He will speak to man through His Word, the Bible, which is illuminated by the Holy Spirit, not through extra-biblical revelation. He will not add anything or take anything away from the pages of Scripture through special revelation.[113] I believe this move toward special revelation is a dangerous progression. God will speak and illuminate His Word, and we have the ability to understand it. We do not need any insider wisdom or special revelation, but rather we can read it and understand it for ourselves, as the Holy Spirit brings illumination to its meaning and interpretation.

Another way in which the NAR practices extra-biblical revelation is prophecy. Groups of prophetic leaders in the NAR have come together to form what they call "prophetic councils." These prophetic councils examine information that they deem to be prophetic in nature. The several different councils assemble prophetic utterances that are accumulated from various sources from within the broader NAR. The most influential of these councils worldwide is the Apostolic Council of Prophetic Elders (ACPE). This council, convened by Cindy Jacobs, pub-

---

112 *John 16:13; 17:17 (ESV)*

113 *Rev. 22:18-19 (ESV)*

lishes a yearly compilation of prophetic utterances which they call the "Word of the Lord." The council publishes this document in Charisma Magazine among other places. Some prophets that sit on this council have claimed that they prophesied world events such as the September 11 terrorist attacks, the financial catastrophe of 2008, and other political and natural disasters in the last several years (to read more on the NAR office of Prophet refer to Douglas Geivett and Holly Pivec's book, *A New Apostolic Reformation?*).[114] I do not want to intimate that the gift of prophecy no longer exists. However, to name this prophetic document in which they predict world events "The Word of the Lord," it leads me to believe that they are making their prophetic document tantamount to scripture. This is a quintessential extra-biblical revelation.

The Bible, when translated correctly, seeks to stay as close to the original languages as possible. That is what a translation is. The goal of a translation should be to express the meaning of the original author into another language that you are translating into. One should not add things that are not at all intended or explicitly written by the original authors. The ESV, for instance, has as its purpose, "to be transparent to the original text, letting the reader see as directly as possible the structure and meaning of the original."[115] All commissioned Bible translation projects that are reliable and reputable are carefully done with large teams of experts so as to avoid errors. For instance, the ESV, a more recent translation has a translation oversight committee that was made up of fourteen of the world's experts in their field or section of the Bible. The translation review consisted of fifty more leading scholars, and the

---

114   Geivett, R. Douglas., and Holly Pivec., *A New Apostolic Reformation?: A Biblical Response to a Worldwide Movement*, (WOOSTER, OHIO: WEAVER Book Company, 2014). Kindle location 1939-1957

115   "About the ESV", Translation Philosophy, Accessed on November 13, 2016, http://www.esv.org/about/translation-philosophy/

advisory council was made up of fifty-four of the world's leading scholars to approve the final draft. In other words, there could not have been any egregious errors when translating through a host of redactors.

Another development in the NAR that could prove tenuous for defending their practice of "Extra-Biblical Revelation" is the commissioning of a new translation of the Bible. It is called *"The Passion Translation."* It is written by Brian Simmons, and it is endorsed by many NAR leaders including, Apostle Ché Ahn and Bill Johnson among others.[116] On first glance, one of the enormous problems with this "legitimate translation" as it has been named, is that it has been done by one person. In all other acknowledged modern translations, as with the ESV, they have been done by a large cohort as to avoid any mistakes. The second concern I have is that there are many overreaches and inaccuracies in the text with the translation, even the English has mistakes.[117]

Simmons seeks many times to incorporate ideas into his translation like "Kingdom Now" Theology among other NAR teachings. Things are included in the translation by Simmons that are nowhere even intonated by the Biblical authors. For instance, adding to greetings in Paul's letters things that he did not write.[118] Even a paraphrase like the well-known *The Message* by Eugene H. Peterson was edited and compared by many different scholars. For instance, when I was in seminary, one of

---

116   "A New Bible: The Passion Translation", on April 22, 2013, "The Elijah List", Accessed November 13, 2016, http://www.elijahlist.com/words/display_word.html?ID=12057

117   "What's wrong with the Passion "Translation"?", on January 6 2016, Andrew Wilson, Accessed on November 13, 2016, http://thinktheology.co.uk/blog/article/whats_wrong_with_the_passion_translation

118   Refer to Holly Pivec's 4-part series called "A New NAR Bible – 'The Passion Translation'", on April 26, 2013, Holly Pivec, Accessed November 13, 2016, http://www.spiritoferror.org/2013/04/a-new-nar-bible-the-passion-translation/3014

my Old Testament professors had a few chapters of *The Message* that he was correcting. This particular professor was one of the foremost Old Testament scholars in the world. Even so, Peterson does not claim to have a translation, but rather a paraphrase, and seeks to stay true to the ideas of the Biblical authors. He just puts things into everyday language.

When *The Passion Translation* is held up in comparison with a highly accurate translation such as the ESV, the NAR influence becomes evident. For example, Galatians 2:19 reads, "For through the law I died to the law, so that I might live to God."[119] *The Passion Translation* reads, "It was when I tried to obey the law that I was condemned with a curse, because I'm not able to fulfill every single detail of it. But because the Messiah lives in me, I've now died to the law's *dominion* over me so that I can live for God in *heaven's* (emphasis added) freedom!"[120] Besides the error of verbosity of the translation, the emphasis on Dominionism comes through unmistakably. Even though the word or idea of "dominion" is nowhere in the Greek, Simmons inserts it here. The Textus Receptus Greek version of Galatians 2:19 reads "ἐγὼ γὰρ διὰ νόμου νόμῳ ἀπέθανον ἵνα θεῷ ζήσω"[121] the normal words that are translated as "dominion," or "dominions," are three different Greek words either "ἐξουσία" (pronounced ex-oo-see'-ah), "κράτος" (pronounced krat'-os), or "κυριότης" (pronounced koo-ree-ot'-ace). I am not a linguist. I only had my share of Greek in Bible College and Seminary, but it is relatively obvious that the way this verse is translated is incorrect. Simmons introduces the word "dominion" when none of the three Greek words typically translated as "dominion" appear in this verse.

---

119   *Galatians 2:19 (ESV)*

120   *Simmons, Brian. Letters From Heaven By the Apostle Paul (The Passion Translation), BroadStreet Publishing, 2014, kindle version.*

121   *"Galatians 2:19" accessed May 22, 2017,*
http://biblehub.com/text/galatians/2-19.htm

Another example of translation overreach is Galatians 6:6. The ESV translates it, "Let the one who is taught the word share all good things with the one who teaches."[122] *The Passion Translation* reads, "And those who are taught the Word will receive an *impartation* (emphasis added) from their teacher; a sharing of wealth takes place between them".[123] Another buzzword in the NAR is "impartation." Impartations are frequently conferred or bestowed on people by one who is a prophet or apostle. In NAR terms the word impartation refers to the prophet or apostle imparting the Holy Spirit anointing to the receptor. In other words, the impartation of the same gifting of power for miracles will be conferred on the recipient of the impartation. So, in NAR understanding if you hang around prophets and apostles long enough you get the same degree of power and Holy Spirit ministry. Again, blatantly, nowhere in Paul's Greek is a word that could even reasonably be translated as "impartation." The Greek word κοινωνέω (pronounced koy-no-neh'-o) could only realistically be translated to "share with others, communicate, distribute, or to be a partaker." A few other examples of translation malfeasance with *The Passion Translation* are, the inclusion of theologically significant NAR jargon that do not appear in the New Testament Greek that they are translated from. NAR vernacular like "realm," "destiny," and "abundance," appear in *The Passion Translation*.[124]

The Passion Translation has been funded and promoted by the NAR and from an Apostle of the NAR who has no expertise outside of working on a translation of an African language with New Tribes Mission. Simmons seems to have no other significant expertise in Bib-

---

122 *Galatians 6:6 (ESV)*

123 *Simmons, Brian. Letters From Heaven By the Apostle Paul*
(The Passion Translation), BroadStreet Publishing, 2014, kindle version.

124 *"The Passion Translation: The Bible of Bethel and the NAR" accessed May 22,*
2017, http://saraboyd.org/?p=309

lical languages outside of that. Those who work on translations should have some higher degree in linguistics, especially when they are the sole translator. Simmons does not claim to have a degree in any field of linguistics.[125] According to *The Passion Translation* website, his doctoral degree was received from Wagner Leadership Institute with a specialization on prayer.[126] This school has deep NAR ties and was started by well-known Apostle C. Peter Wagner.

This translation attempt creeps extremely close to cults that have commissioned their own translations of the Bible. For Instance, Jehovah's Witnesses *(New World Translation)*, and Mormons (*Book of Mormon* and their own Bible translation). All of which have serious errors, and have done their translations with a bend toward their theology. Many cult leaders who commissioned Bible translations claimed direct visitations from Jesus Christ, angels, or had visions, or dreams. In a sermon at Healing Waters Church in Selden, New York, Simmons claimed, "I had a visitation. I was given the commission by the Lord, as He breathed on me, and released me, and called me to translate the Bible."[127]

He also vaguely explained additional angelic visitations and dreams that revealed to him that he should translate the Bible. Furthermore,

---

125 "Apostle Brian Simmons' Love/Hate Relationship With Scholarship and Academic Degrees", on June 28, 2013, Holly Pivec, Accessed November 13, 2016, http://www.spiritoferror.org/2013/06/apostle-brian-simmons-lovehate-relationship-with-scholarship-and-academic-degrees/3513

126 "FAQs: What is The Passion Translation and who is behind it?," accessed March 10, 2017, https://www.thepassiontranslation.com/faqs/

127 "BRIAN SIMMONS - "Song of Solomon" Part 1," YouTube Viseo, 14:05, February 19, 2012, posted by "HealingWatersNY," Accessed March 10, 2017, https://www.youtube.com/watch?v=H8pmNZnlzIA

he said that his wife has four dreams a night and thousands of interpreted dreams, many of which reveal that Jesus has commissioned his translation work. One tell-tale sign of a new movement that wants to support its own theology is one that produces its own Bible translation, adding elements that were never meant by the Biblical authors. This is the embodiment of "Extra-Biblical Revelation," and flirts too closely to cult tendencies.

We can protect ourselves against "Extra-Biblical Revelation" by knowing and being highly familiar with the word of God, to be able to divide truth from error. We can also be warned about such projects like this that seek to bend the meaning of the original Biblical authors. I heard recently a preacher that used *The Passion Translation*. It was quite easy for me to spot the errors in this translation that had added meaning that was not in the original text. I referred right away to the Greek text in a cell phone application to check because I was not entirely sure. I discovered from the Greek text that the embellishments and additions were staggering. If I was not sure about what I heard, then how is the regular church member able to discern the differences?

The additions pointed to a Dominionist or "Kingdom Now" perspective. To the untrained ear, it sounds wonderful that God would be such a God that would desire for Heaven to invade earth. However, these additions do not appear in the original ancient manuscripts. I could be mistaken in my assessment, but it seems reasonably clear, that Bill Johnson, Cindy Jacobs, Ché Ahn, Brian Simmons and other Apostles of the NAR are bending truth and even the words of Scripture to their meaning, and in so doing, propagate these new-fangled extra-biblical teachings. It is helpful for us to continue to put scripture to memory so that we can guard against any seed of false teaching that might grow up in our hearts over and against God's written revealed word.

CHAPTER SUMMARY

Extra-biblical revelation is any information or content outside the Bible either in the form of knowledge or experience which gives us information concerning God, His work or His will, which is not directly from the Bible.

Hermeneutics is the science of Biblical interpretation.

Eisegesis is super-imposing a meaning onto a biblical text that the writers did not intend.

Exegesis is the proper practice of drawing the meaning out of the text.

The NAR has established "Prophetic Councils" to publish the yearly prophetic publications, one being "The Word of the Lord."

The NAR has commissioned its own Bible translation called *"The Passion Translation."* It is written by Brian Simmons who has no linguistic expertise, and includes NAR Theological perspectives that were not included by the original biblical authors.

Protecting ourselves against extra-biblical revelation includes knowing the Bible so well that we can discern truth from error.

DIVERGENT THEOLOGY

DOMINIONISM

"Jesus shall reign where'er the sun does his successive journeys run; His kingdom stretch from shore to shore, till moons shall wax and wane no more."
— Isaac Watts (1719)

Dominionism is a theological school of thought that says that God gave Adam and Eve dominion over the earth and that Satan usurped man's dominion through the Fall. Christ defeated Satan and took back dominion of the earth on the cross. He gave dominion back to believers to re-establish dominion through the inception of the Kingdom of God on this earth. Then and only then can Jesus return, when we have ushered in the kingdom of God through dominion. Johnson writes,

> Has it ever occurred to you that one of your jobs on earth is … to prove the will of God? Your calling and my calling as believers may be too massive to fully understand, but the Bible's command is clear: Our job is to demonstrate that the reality that exists in Heaven can be manifested right here, right now. We are not just to be people who believe the right things about God, but people who put the will of God on display, expressing it and causing others to realize, "oh so that's what God is like." … Jesus taught and demonstrated that the Kingdom of God is a present tense reality—it exists now in the invisible realm and is superior to everything in the visible realm.[128]

This is, of course, a total misinterpretation of Romans 12:1-2. The Greek word for "prove" is δοκιμάζω, which transliterated is pronounced

---

[128] Johnson, Bill, *The Supernatural Power of a Transformed Mind 40-Day Devotional and Personal Journal* (Shippensburg: Destiny Image Publishing Inc., 2011), 3

"dokimadzo." It means to test by implication, to approve, allow or discern, or examine, prove, or try.[129] This passage is saying that through non-conformity to this world, and by renewing your mind through the Scriptures, you will be able to know the will of God. We will be able to understand it and recognize what God wants us to do. This is poor hermeneutics and exegesis from Johnson, however right in line with Dominionist Theology. "On earth, as it is in Heaven" is a central vision for life and ministry at Bethel Church, which lines up with Dominionist theology also known as "Kingdom Now" theology. Johnson describes this in further detail:

> God's idea was to have a planet engulfed in His glorious rule, with mankind flawlessly "proving the will of God" on earth as it is in Heaven … Of course, we know the original plan got derailed, and that Adam forfeited the rulership God gave him over the earth, putting humanity into slavery to the enemy … In the death and resurrection of Jesus Christ, God took back the authority man had given away and reclaimed our purpose on this earth … We, the Church, are called to extend His rule in this earthly sphere, just as Adam was called to do.[130]

This is almost a word for word explanation of what Dominionism teaches. This is another fallacious teaching on the Fall and human depravity. This is nowhere near biblical. This form of theology should be resisted. If we took this teaching at face value, then the natural outcome would be striving for Theocratic (God as King) forms of government, before Jesus will be able to return to earth.

---

129   Thomas, Robert L., *New American Standard Exhaustive Concordance of the Bible: Including Hebrew-Aramaic and Greek Dictionaries* (Holman Bible Pub, 1981)

130   Johnson, Bill, *The Supernatural Power of a Transformed Mind Expanded Edition: Access to a Life of Miracles* (Shippensburg: Destiny Image Publishers Inc., 2014), 30

So, let me explain what is wrong with this theological perspective. First, did Adam "give away" his authority; or rather disobey a holy God, thus falling into sin? Adam did not give away authority, but rather fell into sin. God ultimately has His sovereign rule over the universe to this day despite the Fall. Additionally, Christ will continue to enact His sovereign rule over every corner of the universe.

Colossians 1:15-20 describes a completely sovereign Christ who has not relinquished His authority to Adam, nor Satan, nor any other created being. Although Johnson wrongly claims that God's plan got "derailed," we know God continues to work His sovereign redeeming plan throughout history. As the great Dutch reformer Abraham Kuyper once said, "There is not a square inch in the whole domain of our human existence over which Christ, who is Sovereign over all, does not cry: 'Mine!'"[131]

The truth is that we have never seen anything in our lives that God didn't create and continue to sustain by the power of His Word (Revelation 4:11, Col 1:15-20). Christ is personally involved in maintaining and sustaining the existence of everything that is in our field of vision at this very instant (Hebrews 1:3). Everything that we see, along with every person who beholds creation, were made by and through Christ. We were made for one ultimate reason: to belong to and 'be unto' Christ (Col 1:16). As the *Westminster Shorter Catechism* espouses, "Man's chief end is to glorify God, and to enjoy Him forever."[132] Anything short of this chief end is not fulfilling the purposes that God had in mind for man.

---

131   Bratt, James D., ed., *Abraham Kuyper: A Centennial Reader* (Grand Rapids: Eerdmans, 1998), 488

132   Boyd, James R., *The Westminster Shorter Catechism: With Analysis, Scriptural Proofs, Explanatory and Practical Inferences, and Illustrative Anecdotes* (Philadelphia: Presbyterian Board of Publication and Sabbath-school Work, 1854)

Dominionism is a core teaching of the NAR and most prevalent in Johnson's individual books. I read through all his books. The themes in each book were mostly the same. His first theme usually goes something like this. Jesus is not God (or somehow laid aside His divinity) otherwise, we would not be able to do the things He did (because we are not God). Second, we were created for Dominion over the earth. We gave up Dominion when we agreed with Satan in opposition to the Dominion of God on this earth. Thirdly, as the church, we should be working to regain that Dominion that Adam and Eve misplaced. Thus, miracles, manifestations, and Heaven invading earth is the return to that Dominion that God originally desired. Johnson describes his view very meticulously in his book *When Heaven Invades Earth*:

> Man was created in the image of God and placed in the Father's ultimate expression of beauty and peace: The Garden of Eden. Outside of that Garden it was a different story. It was without the order and blessing contained within and was in great need of the touch of God's delegated one — Adam ... But in Genesis chapter 1 we discover it's not a perfect universe. Satan had rebelled and had been cast out of Heaven, and with him a portion of the fallen angels took dominion of the earth. It's obvious why the rest of the planet needed to be subdued—it was under the influence of darkness (Genesis 1:2). God could have destroyed the devil and his host with a word, but instead He chose to defeat darkness through His delegated authority—those made in His image who were lovers of God by choice.[133]

One of the major errors of this statement is that the darkness described in Genesis 1:2, Johnson takes to mean a spiritual darkness that

---

133 Johnson, Bill, *When Heaven Invades Earth: A Practical Guide to a Life of Miracles* (Shippensburg: Treasure House, 2003), 30

Satan somehow controlled. He teaches all this about Satan controlling everything outside of the garden of Eden without any Biblical substantiation, but rather overreaching textual speculation. Johnson makes commentary on the text that is not there and goes against historical interpretations of Genesis. Scripture never alludes to this teaching that Satan had control of the world outside the garden before The Fall. The darkness in Genesis 1:2 is obviously referring to the sequence of creation; the period in which there was an absence of light. Genesis 1:2 describes a physical darkness and in Genesis 1:3, God said: "let there be light." Furthermore, in Genesis 1:2, there was chronologically not a Garden of Eden yet, so how could darkness have ruled outside the garden when it had not yet been created? This whole teaching bases itself on one word and a very poor interpretation of the text.

Moreover, The General Council of the Assemblies of God, a major Pentecostal denomination, in a paper entitled *Endtime Revival—Spirit-Led and Spirit-Controlled: A Response Paper to Resolution 16* condemned Dominionism and "Kingdom Now" theology and teaching saying, "This *errant* (emphasis added) theology says that Jesus will not return until the Church takes dominion of the earth back from Satan and his followers."[134] Within this paper, many of the NAR teachings are also named "deviant" such as "Manifest Sons of God," "Joel's Army," the Prosperity Gospel (WOF) and "Generational Curses." The Assemblies of God General Council pleads with churches to demonstrate extreme caution when discerning physical manifestations seen in the NAR and so-called revivals.

---

134   *"Endtime Revival-Spirit-Led and Spirit-Controlled" August 11, 2000, General Council of the Assemblies of God, accessed November 3, 2016, https://ag.org/Beliefs/Topics-Index/Revival-Endtime-Revival--Spirit-Led-and-Spirit-Controlled*

It is also important to note that many of these NAR leaders and churches such as Bethel in Redding have left the Assemblies of God, or broken all denominational ties or affiliations. In January of 2006, Bethel made their exit from the Assemblies of God denomination. In a letter posted on their website after their exit from the denomination, Johnson wrote that their leaving was:

> not a reaction to conflict but a response to a call ... we feel called to create a network that helps other networks thrive — to be one of many ongoing catalysts in this continuing revival. Our call feels unique enough theologically and practically from the call on the Assemblies of God that this change is appropriate.[135]

In his statement, Johnson says clearly that their call felt unique enough theologically to part ways with the Assemblies of God. This is quite possibly true because they were unique from the Assemblies of God, as seen in the General Council's condemnation of one of the pillars of Johnson's and Bethel's teaching, which is Dominionism and "Kingdom Now" theology. If the world's largest Pentecostal denomination (67 million members) names Dominionism and these other divergent theological perspectives as problematic, and many NAR churches have left for the denomination's stand, then it becomes clear who is divergent. Certainly, not just the one Charismatic theological camp has come out against these new teachings. Much of modern Christendom is wholeheartedly opposed to Dominionism.[136]

---

135 Poloma, Margaret M. & Green, Margaret M., *The Assemblies of God: Godly Love and the Revitalization of American Pentecostalism* (NY: NYU Press, 2010), 202

136 "The Assemblies of God and the NAR" June 1, 2013, Holly Pivec, Accessed November 3, 2016,

http://www.spiritoferror.org/2013/06/the-assemblies-of-god-and-the-nar/3246

Dominionism is so heinous and dangerous because it gives Satan more power than he has, and gives man more authority than he deserves. Satan is a defeated foe, a helpless pawn, a slithering beheaded snake. We are sinners saved by grace, brought into sonship, and given an inheritance in the saints. Additionally, we did nothing to deserve or earn what we have received in Christ. Disparately, God is supremely sovereign; He has not relinquished control of this world to anyone. God never loses control of anything, ever; from eternity past to the present, and on into the future. Everything is under His sovereign control, galaxies and the endless reaches of space, this earth and everything on it, countries, governments, armies, all of nature from the top of Mt. Everest to the deepest part of the ocean at the bottom of the Mariana Trench; He is sovereign over all plants and animals, over all movements of the Earth, and even over natural disasters. He is sovereign over all forms of knowledge and understanding, over education and universities, no matter what they do or do not teach. He is supreme over man's scholarship, science, research, and all informational systems. He is absolutely supreme over those things that we will one day discover and those things that we would never uncover even if we had thousands of millennia to do so.[137] Dominionism cannot be true for all of Scripture to describe in such precise detail the loving control that God continually exhibits over the smallest minutiae of creation up to solving the biggest problems in our universe. As the earliest Christian creed claimed, "Jesus is Lord."[138]

---

137 "The Supremacy of Christ (Sermon Jam) – John Piper," YouTube Video, on March 26, 2014, posted by "Truth Endures," Accessed November 5, 2016, https://www.youtube.com/watch?v=VeKgfUGtcI0

138 Col 1:15-20; Heb 1;1-4; Job 1:12; 2:6 Ps 19:1-6; Ps 135:6; Is 43;13; 1 Tim 1:17; 6:15; Rev 15:3; 19:5 (ESV)

CHAPTER SUMMARY

Dominionism teaches that God gave Adam and Eve dominion over the earth and that Satan usurped man's dominion through the Fall

The General Council of the Assemblies of God has condemned Dominionism and Kingdom Now Theology as errant. They also named "Joel's Army," "Manifest sons of God," "Prosperity Gospel," and "Generational Curses" as deviant

Bethel Church in 2006 removed itself from the Assemblies of God Denomination

Colossians 1:15-20 describes Christ's continued sovereignty over everything. He has not relinquished dominion of this earth to Satan, Adam, or any other being. Jesus rules and continues to reign.

"HOSTING THE PRESENCE" OR NEO-GNOSTICISM

The depth of your worship life is a litmus test for your spiritual maturity. If you spend little time in worship and giving God worth with your words, with your life, with your body, with your music, with your song, with your writing, with your pocket book, with your heart, with your soul, with your mind, and everything you are, then I could say with a high degree of certainty, you are a spiritually immature Christian. Be mature! Worship!

It is hard to find a category for Johnson's next teaching but maybe in the neighborhood of Gnosticism. He even wrote a book with the same title *Hosting the Presence: Unveiling Heaven's Agenda*. In another of his books, *Manifesto for a Normal Christian Life*, he describes the peculiar practice of hosting God's presence. It is so strange that it can only be described in his own words.

> Jesus models, better than anyone in Scripture, how to host the presence of the Lord. I would remind you that, obviously, Jesus is God. He is eternal. He is not a created being but he emptied himself and became a man and learned how to host the presence of the Lord. Jesus himself said that he set aside his divinity. The Scriptures tell us that he emptied himself. He could do nothing of himself. None of the miracles did he do as God. He did them all as a man, yielded to God. They are all expressions of a life under the influence of the Holy Spirit. Jesus learned to host the presence of the Lord and in doing so was so conscious of God upon him that when a woman touched his clothing he could tell power had been released from him.

> Imagine being so aware of the Spirit of God on you that, even though you have conversations going on with people around you, even though there is a crowd pushing in around you and touching you, when one person that touches you in faith and there is a withdrawal from your account of presence, or power, you are so conscious of what you are carrying that you realize presence has been released through you. It wasn't because the presence in him was depleted, because the Spirit of God was given to him without measure. It was just that he could tell that there had been a demand put upon what he carried.[139]

In this passage, Jesus was not God and human simultaneously, again Johnson's Christological divergence continues. Actually, it is confusing because he starts off saying Jesus is God and eternal but then goes on to teach that Jesus laid aside His divinity so that He could take back divinity (or presence of the Holy Spirit) again. That doesn't make logical sense. Why not, if you were Jesus, just keep your divinity so you wouldn't have to do all this difficult "laying aside" and taking back the Holy Spirit presence exchange? If you were God, why not just stay God? This is confusing, and at a minimum, careless language. Also, here is a mishandling of the Scripture. Jesus never said that "presence" went out from Him, but rather that "power" went out from Him. Because Jesus said "power" went out from Him, that clearly displays that Jesus had complete command of His holy power. One could conclude from Johnson's teaching that Jesus did not have control and authority over His holy attributes and power.

Further, Johnson said that Jesus could tell that there had been a "demand" put on what He had carried. This is so unchristian it is hard to

---

139 Johnson, Bill, *Manifesto for a Normal Christian Life: The HTB Talks Kindle Edition* (Redding: Bill Johnson Ministries, 2013), Sample pages

know where to start. God never has a "demand" put on His glory or presence. In most cases, when the glory of the Lord was revealed in the Scriptures, either people were dead, wanted to be dead, or were on their faces hoping they would not soon be dead.

All jokes aside, God never had any demands placed on the scope or extent of His glory. He is God, and nothing is too demanding of His power or glory. Nothing. Having a demand placed on the presence of God sounds more like New Age, Eastern Mysticism, or Occult-like, than Christian. The gods of those religions are confined to time and space and are not omniscient, omnipotent, or omnipresent. Demands could be put on other gods/spirits because they are limited. The spirits of these other religions do have demands placed on their power and sovereignty that they cannot meet. Conversely, the God of Heaven and Earth is absolutely sovereign. The God of the Bible is beholden to no demands placed on Him by any man, or the request of His power! YHWH, the great I AM, has no demand too great for Him. Nonetheless, these practices carry with them all sorts of other dangers and are wholly unchristian. Later on in his book, Johnson describes the practice of "hosting the presence" in more depth:

> And you will always reflect the nature of the world we are most aware of. What you live conscious of is what you will reproduce in the world around you ... The Holy Spirit *upon* (emphasis added) Jesus was the very power which would emanate from him to change and transform people's lives and circumstances. Torments that were on people were broken off, diseases were healed, and hope was given to people who had no hope. Jesus ruined every funeral that he attended – including his own ... They realized that Paul could not go everywhere so they would just take articles of his clothing and take them to a sick or dying or tormented person and they would be set free. It wasn't sim-

ply an act of faith. That would be noble enough in itself. But it was because the Spirit of God can actually saturate cloth. And just the simple residue, the crumbs from the table, was enough to bring deliverance and healing when it was taken from the presence of the Lord ... I don't know how to learn anything but by experimenting. Those people who like to get it right the first time should stay away from the gifts of the Spirit, because we have to learn by experiment, in a context of safety ... When I became conscious of the presence I would walk into the store and then I would start buying whatever I needed. And if what I wanted was in one particular place in the shop I'd walk up and down the other aisles first. I wouldn't go straight to it. I'd walk up and down the aisles, because I felt like I was a sprinkler system walking up and down, watering the entire place with presence.[140]

The error that lies within these words is quite distressing. First, Jesus had the Spirit "upon" Him. It might be just semantics, but the Spirit was not upon Jesus but was rather in Jesus. Spirit is Jesus and Jesus is Spirit. Again, Johnson's basis in the improper Kenosis and Trinitarian theology becomes more defined. Jesus only ministered the presence of and carried the Holy Spirit with Him and somehow shared that presence that was "upon" Him. In Johnson's view, Jesus was not as the great Nicene Creed claims, "God of God, Light of Light, true God of true God, begotten and not made; of the very same nature of the Father, by Whom all things came into being, in heaven and on earth, visible and invisible."[141] The whole creed reads,

---

140   Ibid, *(Sample Pages)*

141   *Schaff, Philip, and David S. Schaff, The Creeds of Christendom: With a History and Critical Notes (Grand Rapids: Baker Book House, 1983)*
Kelly, J. N. D. Early Christian Creeds. (New York: D. McKay Co., 1972), 215-216

We believe in one God, the Father Almighty, Maker of all things visible and invisible. And in one Lord Jesus Christ, the Son of God, begotten of the Father the only-begotten; that is, of the essence of the Father, God of God, Light of Light, very God of very God, begotten, not made, being of one substance (ὁμοούσιον) with the Father; by whom all things were made both in heaven and on earth; who for us men, and for our salvation, came down and was incarnate and was made man; he suffered, and the third day he rose again, ascended into heaven; from thence he shall come to judge the quick and the dead. And in the Holy Ghost. But those who say: 'There was a time when he was not;' and 'He was not before he was made;' and 'He was made out of nothing,' or 'He is of another substance' or 'essence,' or 'The Son of God is created,' or 'changeable,' or 'alterable'—they are condemned by the holy catholic and apostolic Church.[142]

It seems like Johnson teaches that Jesus is some sort of cheap knock-off god. This alone is enough to discount every other word Johnson says in his teaching. However, let us examine this quote a little further.

He concludes from Acts nineteen verse twelve, where handkerchiefs were taken from Paul to heal people, that the Spirit of God can saturate a piece of cloth? And the Holy Spirit has a residue? This is an Animistic belief and not Christian. Animism is a tribal religion that says we can manipulate spirits that are in objects. Animism more specifically, refers to a religious system which seeks to deal with encounters with spirit realities in this life, and the spirit realm, with a view to cooperate with that world. God does not indwell or saturate cloths or leave residues. Johnson goes on to say that he knows only how to "experiment" when it comes to the gifts of the Spirit. This experimentation has hidden dan-

---

142 Ibid, 215-216

gers. The obvious danger is that people become open to New Age, Eastern Mysticism, and Animistic practices. The more clandestine dangers are the slow erosion of affection for Christ, and a craving and longing for supernatural phenomena and experiences that are never alluded to in the New Testament.

This culture of experimentation is rubbing off on his congregation also. It seems that Johnson has no problem trying "new" things in experimentation that are off limits for us as Christians. This is where the previously cited practices of glory clouds, gold dust, angel feathers, gems appearing, conjuring angel orbs, fire tunnels, spirit travel, out-of-body experiences, healings, prophecy, portal travel, extra-biblical revelation, raising the dead, new wine movement, drunken glory, visualization, laughter, chanting, soaking, tuning forks, and waking up angels come in. The danger here is that this type of emotionally driven experimentation may open people up to powers that are not from God.

At this point, you may be wondering why you have not come across many of these practices in Scripture. It is because they are not there, and Christ-honoring churches should not practice them. There is nothing in Scripture that makes any of these things something we as Christians should practice or even be open to. Furthermore, these practices are spiritually treacherous for us, because they open our lives up to supernatural forces that the enemy has control over, and God strictly forbids. Johnson later describes himself as a sort of sprinkler of the Holy Spirit where he waters an entire place with presence. This sounds more like a medium (someone who mediates between the Spirit world and the physical world) than the New Testament practice of the ministry of the Holy Spirit.

Paul, in his second letter to Timothy, instructs him in what will happen when people will not endure sound doctrine, but rather, wanting to have their ears tickled, they will surround themselves with teachers that will teach them in accordance with their own desires.[143] Of course, everyone wants a message of prosperity, healing, and wealth. It sounds like a great idea to "sow a seed of faith" (which means give money to a ministry in WOF jargon) so that God will bless me tenfold (That means that God gives a high return on investment)! Everyone wants prosperity, health, and wealth. However, the real message of the Gospel is that of suffering for Christ, "Indeed all who desire to live a godly life in Christ Jesus will be persecuted."[144] Mark 8:34 also shows us the way of the cross that leads to life "If anyone would come after me, let him deny himself and take up his cross and follow me. For whoever would save his life will lose it, but whoever loses his life for my sake and the gospel's will save it (ESV)."

There are so many biblical themes and characters that stand in direct antithesis to almost every prosperity teaching of the WOF, TWM, and NAR that it would be impossible to name them all here. The most glaring example would be Jesus Himself. He stands in opposition to the message of prosperity. He was poor, homeless, rejected, scorned, reviled, forsaken, abandoned by His best friends, and beaten "as one from whom men hide their faces he was despised, and we esteemed him not."[145] His life is the direct antithesis of the message of the prosperity gospel. His glorious and humble life is rather the forsaking of the ways and prosperity of this world, which He had full authority and rights to take unto Himself. Astonishingly, our Lord "humbled himself by becoming obedient to the point of death even death on a cross."[146] This is the bold countercultural message of Christ. This is the wonderful good shepherd that we serve. He loved us unto death, and we can enter into His suffering and as Paul

---

143   *2 Tim. 4:3-4 (ESV)*

144   *2 Tim. 3:12 (ESV)*

145   *Isa. 53:3 (ESV)*

146   *Phil. 2:8 (ESV)*

says, "share in the fellowship of His sufferings becoming like Him in His death."[147] This is not the message of prosperity, but rather the true gospel of a life of freely chosen suffering along with Christ. Will you heed His call to come and die? "For whoever would save his life will lose it, but whoever loses his life for my sake and the gospel's will save it."[148] It will be worth it!

---

147   Phil 3:10 (ESV)
148   Mark 8:35 (ESV)

CHAPTER SUMMARY

Hosting the Presence of God is a teaching of Bill Johnson that says Jesus was the most faithful person to host the presence of God and that if we are faithful to host God's presence, we will be qualified to receive more presence.

Jesus was "God of God, Light of Light, true God of true God, begotten and not made; of the very same nature of the Father, by Whom all things came into being, in heaven and on earth, visible and invisible"

Jesus Himself stands in opposition to the message of prosperity. He was poor, homeless, rejected, scorned, reviled, forsaken, abandoned by His best friends, and beaten. His life is the direct antithesis of the message of the prosperity gospel. His glorious and humble life is rather the forsaking of the ways and prosperity of this world. Our Lord "humbled himself by becoming obedient to the point of death even death on a cross."

DANGER WITHIN MAINSTREAM EVANGELICAL CHRISTENDOM

Why did Israel wander in the Wilderness for forty years?
Rebellion! Their story teaches us how to live at
the end of the age. So, let's not rebel against God.
It is a nefarious proposition.
— 1 Cor 10:5-15; Heb 3:7-19

There is so much more to be said and written about the WOF, TWM, and NAR but what has been presented should suffice for the simple purposes of exposing the teaching of Bill Johnson, Bethel Church, and the NAR teachers who are trying to find their way into Europe and Germany. In all fairness, Bill Johnson has denied any connection to the NAR.[149] Nevertheless, the links are clear. He appeared at the commissioning of Todd Bentley (Lakeland Revival) as an Apostle with other Apostles from the NAR including Ché Ahn, Rick Joyner, and C. Peter Wagner.[150] Johnson has also appeared on several episodes of Morningstar Ministries TV with Rick Joyner, an Apostle in the NAR.

---

149 Jones, Martyn Wendell, "Cover Story: Inside the Popular, Controversial Bethel Church," *Christianity Today* (April 24, 2016), accessed June 2016, http://www.christianitytoday.com/ct/2016/may/cover-story-inside-popular-controversial-bethel-church.html.

150 Todd Bentley's Apostolic and Prophetic Commissioning 1/4," YouTube video, 09:59, on August 28, 2008, posted by "ozricus," accessed June 2016,
https://www.youtube.com/watch?v=pqaoskr5wlc

Ibid., *Todd Bentley's Apostolic and Prophetic Commissioning 2/4,* 09:39,
https://www.youtube.com/watch?v=iVcXMkSrHEQ

Ibid., *Todd Bentley's Apostolic and Prophetic Commissioning 3/4,* 08:19,
https://www.youtube.com/watch?v=QBnnpiV1nlo

Ibid., *Todd Bentley's Apostolic and Prophetic Commissioning 4/4,* 04:08,
https://www.youtube.com/watch?v=VE9IvUsq8Ws

More specifically, Johnson appeared on an episode to restore Todd Bentley back into ministry, after Bentley had an affair and married the woman with whom he'd had the affair, back into ministry alongside Rick Joyner.[151] The website Spirit of Error does a good job documenting Johnson's connection to the NAR.[152]

In doing my research for this book, I read all of Johnson's books and found that he had received many recommendations for his books from such NAR leaders as Rick Joyner, C. Peter Wagner, Ché Ahn, Mike Bickle, and a forward for one of his books was written by a popular conference speaker currently in Europe, Heidi Baker. All of these leaders who have given favorable quotes, and written forwards for Johnson all have NAR ties, and most are so-called Apostles within the movement.

My purpose has been to uncover the false teaching and divergence from mainline Christendom that these movements pose. As a result, it is pretty clear how these movements effectively position themselves as a very real threat to orthodox historically accepted views of Christ and all the heretofore-mentioned theologies. The problems are blatant and clearly stated and published by these teachers.

These teachings were not hard to uncover. They are published works: their own YouTube sermons, interviews, their own websites, documentaries, and blogs where these heresies are published (refer to the Appen-

---

151 "Todd Bentley's restoration with Rick Joyner & Bill Johnson Sermons," YouTube video, 05:55, on April 8, 2015, posted by "SkyLine TV," accessed June 2016, https://www.youtube.com/watch?v=-nzafj0ylRU&list=PLCZFj_Ex2zmrGIi8ndK8tpvuNLqP7Iwwm&index=5

152 "Yes, Bethel Redding and Bill Johnson are part of the New Apostolic Reformation," Spirit of Error, accessed June 2016, http://www.spiritoferror.org/2016/05/yes-bethel-redding-and-bill-johnson-are-part-of-the-new-apostolic-reformation/5858

dix and Annotated Bibliography for further review and deeper study into the WOF, TWM, and NAR). In listening to numerous sermons from Johnson and other NAR teachers for this project, almost all had staggeringly serious errors and deeply flawed false teaching within. All that is necessary is to hold these teachings up to the lens of the Word of God, and a discerning Christian spirit. Finally, let us bring Scripture to bear in on what we ought to do in regard to false teaching and false teachers.

Jude 3-4 says that we ought to contend for the faith and that certain people will creep into the fold and deny our only Master and Lord. Ephesians 4:14 says that we also ought to not be tossed about by every wave of doctrine. The introductory chapters explained in detail the instance where Paul, in 1st Timothy 1:20, handed two people Hymenaeus and Alexander over to Satan so that they would learn not to blaspheme because their false teaching had spread like gangrene. Again, the writers of the New Testament use harsh language and terminology in reference to false teaching. I am not the type of personality to want to confront in such a harsh fashion, but if the word of God treats false teaching so gravely, then we ought to also. Gangrene cannot be allowed to live in the body of a person as if nothing was wrong. It must be cut off, cut out, eliminated and thrown out or it will poison and kill the body of the infected person. False teaching, in the case of Hymenaeus, was false teaching on the resurrection. Paul explained how these teachings needed to be done away with like gangrene.

In the case of the WOF, TWM, and NAR, which propagate manifold heresies and pose many other problems of heteropraxy. We must act, especially in relation to their more egregious errors, especially such as, in their Christological heresies. Hebrews 13:9 says that we should also not be led away by diverse (divergent) and strange teachings. Romans 16:17 says to watch out for those who "cause divisions and create obstacles contrary to the doctrine that you have been taught; avoid them."[153] We should not see how much we could get from their teaching before we call it false. Said differently, if some of their teachings are heretical, then all of their teachings are heretical, and the Bible commands that we avoid them all together. Paul goes on to share in verse eighteen that these teachers do not serve Christ but their own appetites, and by flattery, they deceive the hearts of the naïve. With these movements, particularly Bethel and Johnson, people often argue that we should "take the good and leave the bad." If there is heresy found in anyone's teaching, it is a dangerous proposition to try to take the good and leave the bad, because one might not be able to discern anymore what it true and what is false. The roots of heresy will affect the whole tree, even the fruit.

---

153   Rom. 16:17 (ESV)

CHAPTER SUMMARY

Evangelicalism must protect itself against the WOF, TWM, and NAR, which propagate manifold heresies and pose many other problems of heteropraxy. We must take care especially in relation to the more egregious errors in relation to Christology

The Bible clearly speaks that pastors, elders, and church leaders should take care that theology and teaching are accurate, and if not, we should take swift action to eliminate the false teaching as seen in Paul's case with Hymenaeus and Philetus.

THE MYSTERIOUS WORK OF THE SPIRIT

*"Without the Spirit, we can neither love God
nor keep His commandments."*
— Augustine of Hippo

Up to this point, I have written much on what this movement teaches, and how these beliefs do not seem to line up with historical Creedal Christendom. Now, I would like to tackle with some practicality what it might look like for the Holy Spirit to work in the lives of believers, the Church, and the world. I have come to know the incredible, mysterious, powerful, and wonderful work of the Holy Spirit in my life, and in the lives of those whom I have served, in more than twenty years of ministry experience. I would like to give some possibilities of how the Spirit does work, and how we can experience His ministry to us, the Church. With a few stories, I will illustrate how the Spirit has demonstrated His ministry in my life.

During my time as youth pastor right after Bible College, I became a very good professional youth minister. Our youth ministry was very successful, and we grew a ministry from a handful of students to around fifty regular students. The problem was that I was a good professional youth minister who had a very poor relationship with Christ. I usually only read the Bible and prayed if I was preparing a sermon, or praying in a ministry context. I had wandered away from a deep and personal relationship with God. Because of this wandering, all kinds of influences came into my life. Unaware, I just pressed on not knowing I was experiencing some sort of spiritual oppression.

One night, as I was trailing off to sleep, all of a sudden, I felt an evil presence in the room. It woke me up straightaway. After becoming fully aware, I had a very vile and evil thought. I had no idea where this could have come from. I believed right away that I was being oppressed by some demonic forces. I tried to sit up in bed but could not. It felt as if there was a heavy weight on my chest. I could not move! Right away, I knew I had to do something. The only thing that came to mind was that passage in the book of Jude. The Archangel Michael was disputing with the devil over the body of Moses. In that encounter with Satan, Michael said, "the Lord rebuke you." Michael dared not try to rebuke the devil himself; he asked the Lord to do it. I thought the same thing. I had no spiritual leg to stand on, but the blood of Christ to deliver me. I started saying out loud "by the blood of the Lamb the Lord Jesus rebuke you!" I repeated it over and over again as I felt the evil trying to advance on me. After a while, I felt the thoughts and the presence of evil slowly relent. It lasted several hours until I finally fell asleep from the weariness of the battle.

That experience shook me to the core. I finally woke up to my great spiritual need in pursuing a deeper and steadier personal relationship with the Lord. I repented of the sins which had entangled me in that time. I got serious about living a holy life and walking in the power of the Holy Spirit. He had gotten my attention! I write this story to illustrate how sometimes we must war against spiritual powers as Ephesians 6:12 describes, "For we do not wrestle against flesh and blood, but against the rulers, against the authorities, against the cosmic powers over this present darkness, against the spiritual forces of evil in the heavenly places (ESV)." As Christians, we are meant to battle in the supernatural realm against principalities and powers. However, we are not to wrestle by our own power!

Dominionism teaches that we are given the task to take back Dominion of this earth from Satan. It appears that this theological perspective teaches that God is not necessarily in control of those corners and dark places where the church must surge in and regain control. It seems to me that God is not sovereign within this view. Biblical spiritual warfare has, as a fundamental principle, that God is in complete sovereign control and authority over the powers of darkness as the Archangel Michael realized. This realization determined how Michael fought. This is why Dominionism could be not just tenuous theologically, but additionally, could work itself out in wrong practices. If God is not in sovereign control of the darkness, then we have an enemy who might not bow the knee to our advances in the name of Jesus. I previously described that Dominionism teaches that we must take back territory from the enemy because we relinquished dominion or "agreed with Satan" against God in the Fall. However, this is not a Biblical teaching, and could seriously affect how we approach spiritual warfare.

When my brother was seventeen, he got into a life-threatening car accident. He had broken his right leg, both arms and wrists, his right knee was shattered, and had many other facial and cosmetic injuries. His car had been peeled open like a tuna can by a rather large tree. I saw the car, and it was hard to believe that anyone could have lived through what I saw. The tree struck him in the head, and he had broken his neck. He also had significant bleeding on his brain. When I first saw him in the intensive care unit, I would not have recognized him if my mother had not been standing beside his bed. He was badly disfigured. He had twenty-six staples holding his head together. The bleeding on the brain was touch and go for quite a few days. But we believe, through concerted prayer for him, by maybe thousands of people, that God stopped that bleeding on his brain.

He came through those challenging first few days to find out about two weeks later that he had broken his odontoid vertebrae. This vertebra is the same one that famous actor Christopher Reeves broke in his horsing accident. If you break your odontoid vertebrae and your spinal cord is touched, you would become a quadriplegic and would be paralyzed from the neck down. God saved my brother several times from certain death in the hospital. He also protected him from his vertebrae touching his spinal cord. He even lay in the hospital for two weeks before the doctors even knew that he had broken his neck.

After his initial recovery, he had to have three surgeries on his neck. One was called odontoid pin surgery where one of the top neurosurgeons in America tried to place a pin inside his odontoid vertebrae to reattach it to his other vertebrae. Three months after that surgery, the doctor announced to him that the surgery had not worked. The doctor had done thirteen of these same procedures. All of his other odontoid procedures had worked. They then decided on a procedure where hip bone powder was placed in the gap so that the odontoid could fuse to the other vertebrae. That one was successful.

This story illustrates God's all-powerful protecting and healing work. God healed my brother! We prayed, and prayed, and prayed some more. We asked the elders to come and anoint him with oil, and lay hands on him in prayer as prescribed in James 5. Today, he is healed! He is even a little taller because of the various surgeries. He can't turn his neck the whole way, and his knee always hurts right before it rains. He is healed by the mighty power of God, but it didn't happen like we would have liked or suspected healing should go. The way I would have healed him would have been immediate. I would have had him stand up in the ICU and walk out totally whole the way he was right before his wreck, but God had other plans. His plans were that we look to Him as our only help and hope to get us as a family through the "valley of the shadow of death." His plans were to sustain my brother, and also preserve his life (Jeremiah 29:11). He did it, He does it, and He continues to preserve my brother's life, so long as He needs him on this earth. We trust in the eternal physician, and even now more because of what we went through with my brother.

This is just one example of how the sustaining healing power of God works. He does heal and restore people. Sometimes, He heals through immediate healing, through physicians, medicine, and other times through natural restoration that He has set up in the creation order. I do not see any scriptural grounds, however, that God heals as a rule, or as previously stated through the atonement of Christ. Healing and miracles can help us draw near to Christ, but they are not our key faith driver, the word of God is. Tim Chester and Steve Timmis write in their book, *Total Church*:

> There is a kind of faith that comes from seeing miraculous signs, but true faith comes through the words of Scripture and the words of Jesus. John goes on: 'now while he was in Jerusalem at the Passover feast, many people saw the miraculous signs he was doing and believed in his name. But Jesus would not entrust himself to them, for he knew all men' (knew the hearts of men) (verses 23-24). Jesus does not trust the kind of faith that comes from seeing miraculous signs. It is not difficult to imagine why. Such faith is likely to be fair-weather faith. It will believe when signs are performed, prayers are answered, things are going well. But it is not the sort of faith that will survive the loss of a child, a period of illness or some other trauma. Persevering faith comes through the word of God.[154]

Look at the normative response to healing in the New Testament. The responses were almost always repentance, faith, worship, following Jesus, discipleship, and obedience to the Lord. In other words, people responded to the gospel! Healing didn't happen for the sake of healing, but for the sake of the gospel. Jesus never healed just because it was

---

154   Chester, Tim, and Steve Timmis, *Total Church: A Radical Reshaping around Gospel and Community* (Wheaton, IL: Crossway Books, 2008). 27

good. He healed because He was good. And He didn't walk away afterward leaving people to themselves. Through healing, Jesus always called people to repentance, faith, and following after Him. Healing was one way Jesus helped people turn their faces to Him. Nevertheless, healing did not always turn people to Christ. Think of the ten lepers, only one returned to thank Jesus. The other nine were healed of a crippling devastating skin disease, but only one returned and set his face to worship Jesus. That is the limitation of healing it does not always produce faith.

During this long drawn out situation with my brother, Jesus used the difficulty and the healing to gently help us look toward Him, to trust in Him, lean on Him, to cast all our cares on Him. He answered with a resounding yes! I'm your good shepherd! His rod and His staff led us faithfully through the "valley of the shadow of death."

I have been involved in many churches and denominations in my time in ministry, Baptist, Presbyterian, Free Evangelical, Charismatic, Methodist, Evangelical Covenant, etc. Although I do not waffle theologically, I have preached and ministered alongside dear brothers and sisters in Christ on almost every Evangelical spectrum. I respect and admire them all. While I was a youth pastor in California, we partnered for many years with a Methodist Charismatic church in East Germany. We assisted them by helping put on English Camps to minister to and reach teenagers with the gospel in their area. During our times ministering alongside them, I realized how they practiced the wonderful "sign gifts" of the Spirit.

One time, while visiting their church, many people were trying to speak in tongues in a worship service at the same time. Right away, the pastor sought to bring some order. He asked all the people who had a tongue to wait, and we would hear them in turn. He asked for a translation to every other person who had a tongue, and always one after the other. I was very impressed with how God spoke through people, especially those with the gift of translation. The translated messages were very near to some scripture passages that we all needed to hear at that moment. My goals are not to debate Cessationism and Continuationism here. However, if someone were to be a Continuationist, this is how the gift of tongues could and should be practiced in the regular expression of the body of Christ as the Bible clearly defines it should be.[155]

Conversely, I have witnessed how the "sign gifts" have been practiced in a certain type of chaos that the New Testament strictly warns against. As 1st Corinthians 14:33 explains in reference to the expression of the sign-gifts, "For God is not a God of confusion but of peace. As in all the churches of the saints (ESV)." Whether or not you believe that the sign gifts have ceased today (Cessationism), I do think we could all agree that the sign gifts should, at the very least, be practiced as the Bible explains they should be.

Furthermore, I believe that I have the biblical gift of prophecy and discernment. I have never been able to prophesy about a specific future event. My prophetic voice is usually exhibited in foretelling the truth and speaking it into difficult situations that need some truth shed on them. I often seek, with that gift, to specifically lead the Church to a deeper obedience and truth. For example, in writing this book, I believe I am practicing my gift of prophecy and discernment in tandem. These are a few ways that the Holy Spirit has specifically applied my spiritual gifts to edify His church.

To help us further understand the mysterious, powerful, and wonderful work of the Spirit, I want to share a few ways He works in believers, the church, and the world. First and foremost, the Holy Spirit works

---

[155] *1 Corinthians 14:1-40; 1 Corinthians 12:1-31;*

to glorify and reveal Jesus to the world by turning men's hearts towards Christ (John 16:14). In that way, He works powerfully and supernaturally (1Corinthians 2:14). He works through believers by giving them spiritual gifts (Romans 12; 1 Corinthians 12; Ephesians 4). He works in an orderly fashion, not in chaos and disorderliness (1 Corinthians 14:33). He works in ways so that we receive the message, and the message of the Spirit is to convict people of sin and guilt (John 16:8). He works by coming alongside believers to empower them (named the "Helper" in John 16:7). He indwells believers and seals them unto salvation until the day of redemption (Ephesians 1:13; 4:30; 1 Corinthians 3:16-17). He fills people with Himself to live sanctified lives (Ephesians 5:18; Galatians 5:16-21). In other words, a filled and indwelled believer will live a holy, sanctified, and victorious life over sin. He leads us into all truth (John 16:13). He comforts us and doesn't leave us alone like orphans (John 14:18; 2 Corinthians 1:4). The Spirit gives us words to pray when we have not the words. He groans with us with groans too deep for words (Romans 8:26-27). The Spirit will never lead us to do anything that would contradict the Scripture. Lastly, He works into believers the fruit of the Spirit (Galatians 5:22-23).

I don't claim to have experienced all the ways that the Holy Spirit works in believers, the church, and the world. I also don't claim that I even know all the ways that the Holy Spirit works. That is the mystery. This list that I have accumulated of ways that the Bible teaches that the Holy Spirit works is neither exhaustive. I share a few of my stories and lists of the Holy Spirit's work to at least give us a minimum framework of how the Holy Spirit does work in the lives of believers, the church, and the world. I do want to be clear. The Holy Spirit will not work in contradiction to this brief list because the scripture reveals that these are the ways He does work. Furthermore, my experience is not authoritative. My experience doesn't validate the scripture; the scripture validates my experience. I want to be faithful to embrace the ways that God has revealed in His word how He does work. In so doing, I embrace the certainty and the mystery of His ways. However, in my opinion, the NAR, TWM, and WOF movements do not practice or teach a biblical ministry of the Holy Spirit.

CHAPTER SUMMARY

My experience with the Holy Spirit doesn't validate the scripture; the scripture validates my experience.

The Bible gives us clear guidance in how the Spirit works in the lives of believers, the Church, and the world. There is a certainty and a mystery to His ways.

DIVERGENT THEOLOGY

INDICTMENT OF FALSE TEACHERS AND PROPHETS

"But false prophets also arose among the people, just as there will be false teachers among you, who will secretly bring in destructive heresies, even denying the Master who bought them, bringing upon themselves swift destruction. And many will follow their sensuality, and because of them the way of truth will be blasphemed. And in their greed they will exploit you with false words. Their condemnation from long ago is not idle, and their destruction is not asleep."
— 2 Peter 2:1–3

2nd Peter 2:1-3 is a powerful indictment against false prophets and teachers. It says that false teachers will rise among the body of Christ. These false teachers will introduce destructive heresies, even denying the Master who bought them (e.g. denying Christ as God). Because of these destructive heresies, the truth will be maligned, and they will exploit you with false words. The end of verse three is one of the most famous verses against false teachers, and it is very strong indeed. "Their judgment from long ago is not idle, and their destruction is not asleep."[156] In other words, God has prepared a day when they will face His judgment, and that judgment will throttle all those false teachers.

This is not an idle threat from God. Their destruction or condemnation is not sleeping. This means that it is active and God is waiting to unleash and activate that coming judgment on them. Paul also writes to Timothy about protecting his doctrine. 1st Timothy 6:3-10 describes how false teachers are conceited. He goes on to say that we must be content with what we have and the love of money is "the root of all kinds

---

156   2 Pet. 2:3 (ESV)

of evil," and some by loving money have "wandered away from the faith and have pierced themselves with many griefs."[157] Why would God have purchased something on the cross (prosperity and material wealth) that Paul says can make us wander away from the faith? That would be ludicrous and counter-intuitive, but Johnson, the WOF, TWM, and NAR teach this in their view of the atonement.

---

157   1 Tim. 6:3-10 (ESV)

CHAPTER SUMMARY

2nd Peter 2:1-3 describes a judgement for false teachers that is not "idle" and their "destruction is not asleep" meaning that God will throttle false teachers with His judgement.

Why would God have purchased something on the cross (prosperity and material wealth) that Paul says can make us wander away from the faith? (1 Timothy 6:3-10)

CONCLUSION

The eternal Christ is truth incarnate! Everything He said, did, and continues to do, was and is totally, absolutely, and irrefutably true forever and always.

"Him we proclaim, warning everyone and teaching everyone with all wisdom, that we may present everyone mature in Christ. For this I toil, struggling with all His energy that he powerfully works within me."
— Colossians 1:28-29

In Conclusion, the Bible tells us clearly through John that we are to test every spirit and not believe everything because there are false prophets in the world. 1st John 4:1-6 gives us clear instructions on false teachings:

> Beloved, do not believe every spirit, but test the spirits to see whether they are from God, for many false prophets have gone out into the world. By this you know the Spirit of God: every spirit that confesses that Jesus Christ has come in the flesh is from God, and every spirit that does not confess Jesus is not from God. This is the spirit of the antichrist, which you heard was coming and now is in the world already. Little children, you are from God and have overcome them, for he who is in you is greater than he who is in the world. They are from the world; therefore they speak from the world, and the world listens to them. We are from God. Whoever knows God listens to us; whoever is not from God does not listen to us. By this we know the Spirit of truth and the spirit of error.[158]

---

[158]   *1 John 4:1-6 (ESV)*

We can clearly see that we are to test every spirit because there are many false prophets in the world. Every spirit that confesses that Jesus Christ is God passes the test. Unfortunately, my dear brothers and sisters in Christ, it grieves me to write to you, but from my research, I have come to the opinion that when the teaching of the WOF, TWM, and NAR including Bill Johnson, Ben Fitzgerald (of Awakening Europe), and Bethel Church in Redding are held up to the lens of Scripture and historical heresies, they do not pass the test. It is my opinion that they are false teachers and should be rebuked as the scriptures command us. All other Christ-honoring Christians should be warned. Consider yourself warned.[159]

In the process of researching and writing this book, I was asked about all the seemingly true healings, exorcisms, and wonders that are supposedly happening in this movement, especially at Bethel. I would like to propose a few ideas as to why evidently legitimate signs, wonders, and miracles are happening. The Bible clearly shows there will be people who navigate in the supernatural with great wonders but they will be rejected by Christ. Jesus Himself explained:

> Beware of false prophets, who come to you in sheep's clothing but inwardly are ravenous wolves. You will recognize them by their fruits. Are grapes gathered from thornbushes, or figs from thistles? So, every healthy tree bears good fruit, but the diseased tree bears bad fruit. A healthy tree cannot bear bad fruit, nor can a diseased tree bear good fruit. Every tree that does not bear good fruit is cut down and thrown into the fire. Thus you will recognize them by their fruits. "Not everyone who says to me, 'Lord, Lord,' will enter the kingdom of heaven, but the one who does the will of my Father who is in heaven. On that day many

---

159   *2 Tim. 4:2; Titus 3:10-11 (ESV)*

will say to me, 'Lord, Lord, did we not *prophesy* in your name, and *cast out demons* in your name, and *do many mighty works* (emphasis added) in your name?' And then will I declare to them, 'I never knew you; depart from me, you workers of lawlessness.'[160]

The Old Testament also comments on prophets who will be able to operate in the supernatural by performing signs and wonders. Deuteronomy 13:1–5 explains how Israel was meant to handle them:

> If a prophet or a dreamer of dreams arises among you and gives you a *sign or a wonder*, and the *sign or wonder* (emphasis added) that he tells you comes to pass, and if he says, 'Let us go after other gods,' which you have not known, 'and let us serve them,' you shall not listen to the words of that prophet or that dreamer of dreams. For the Lord your God is testing you, to know whether you love the Lord your God with all your heart and with all your soul. You shall walk after the Lord your God and fear him and keep his commandments and obey his voice, and you shall serve him and hold fast to him … So you shall purge the evil from your midst.

Independently from Christ's words, this passage in Deuteronomy is another evidence in the Bible that so-called prophets will be able to perform wonders, but in so doing, would seek to draw the people of God away from the worship of the one true God to other gods and divergent theologies. The point of these warnings both from Christ and the Old Testament is that we are not meant to believe the signs because they can be deceptive or originate from sources other than God. Rather, we are to trust and believe the message of the Gospel by the word of God. Only if

---

[160] *Matthew 7:15-23 (ESV)*

the message lines up with the word of God and accepted the teaching of Christendom are we to trust it.

The great reformer Martin Luther likewise commented on "signs and wonders" in a sermon titled, "Christ's Commission to His Disciples to preach the gospel; Christ's Ascension"

> We must not suppose that the signs here mentioned by Christ are all the signs that believers will do, neither must we imagine that all Christians will do them; but Jesus means: All Christians can and may do the signs. Or, if I believe, then am I able to do them; I have the power. Through faith I obtain so much that nothing is impossible to me. If it were necessary and conducive to the spreading of the Gospel, we could do easily the signs; but since it is not necessary, we do not do them. For Christ does not teach that Christians practice the spectacular, but he says they have the power and can do these things. And we have many such promises throughout the Scriptures; for example, in John 14:12, where Christ says: "He that believeth on me, the works that I do shall he do also; and greater works than these shall he do." Therefore, we must allow these words to remain and not gloss them away, as some have done who said that these signs were manifestations of the Spirit in the beginning of the Christian era and that now they have ceased that is not right; for the same power is in the church still. And though it is not exercised, that does not matter; we still have the power to do such signs.[161]

What we can gather from Luther's comments is that signs and wonders are not necessarily normative, or even customary, but rather that

---

161 *Luther, Martin, The Complete Works of Martin Luther: Volume 3, Sermons 42-67 (Delmarva Publications, 2014). Kindle location 3600*

we do have access to and power for signs and wonders through faith to advance the gospel message. That neither means that signs may even be necessary in every gospel situation.

I want to propose three more specific reasons why people are able to operate in the supernatural with signs and wonders, but are false teachers, and rejected by Christ on the day of judgment. First, Christ's name is just that powerful. His name is powerful enough to be used by those who reject Him or are false teachers. In the Book of Acts, chapter twenty-one, there is a story about seven sons of a high priest named Sceva. Other itinerant exorcists were adjuring the name of Jesus by casting out demons. It appears that these exorcists were successful. However, the text gives us the impression that these exorcists were frauds, or at least, only invoking the name of Jesus without being real Christians. We can certainly ascertain from the text that at least, the seven sons of Sceva were frauds. They were going around casting out demons in the name of Jesus whom Paul preaches. On one occasion, a demon answered them by saying, "Jesus I know, and Paul I know, but who are you?" Then the demonized man jumped on the seven men and gave them such a beating that he sent them out of the house bleeding and naked. This biblical story shows us that people are able to operate and perform great signs and wonders, and often with great success, but on occasion, the demons do not recognize those who are seeking to wield the powerful name of Jesus.

The second reason I propose that false teachers are able to exercise power or what seems like Christian miracles is that they are working in the supernatural power of the enemy and attributing the enemy's work to Christ or the name of Christendom. As seen in the previous story of the seven sons of Sceva, they were hucksters, frauds, and counterfeits who were invoking the name of Jesus, but actually, they were operating through the enemy's power. Is there power in Animism, Folk religions, New Age, Necromancy, Fortune Telling, Astrology, Clairvoyance, Sorcery, Witchcraft, and any other Occult powers? Yes, of course, there is, and the Bible strictly forbids us to engage in these practices as previously mentioned.

The third reason I would put forth for why false teachers are able to perform miracles is that they are not miracles at all. There may be some sense that people are healed. In the heat of the moment, maybe they feel better, or are high on adrenaline, or do have some sort of sensation because of the feeling of the emotional high, but are not actually healed of Cerebral Palsy, Cancer, etc. In my research, I have watched hundreds of hours of documentary, and video of so-called healings, and I'm yet to see one that has shown a person who when asked if they were healed from cancer or some other devastating illness has said yes, and given medical evidence to that fact. I could be mistaken, and I am glad to see medical evidence to the contrary. I am yet to encounter any of the medically substantiated evidence they claim to have procured in these movements. This is not to say God does not heal miraculously anymore, He does and can (James 5:13-16). But often, there is no actual healing in the case of these movements. In my pastoral and personal experience, Biblical healing like this takes place behind closed doors with elders praying, as described in James, rather than sensationally on a stage with people parading by so that the faith healer can lay his hand on them.

The question might also be asked of people who are sympathetic to this movement, "aren't we supposed to have emotions and experiences with the Lord?" My answer is a resounding, "Yes!" We are meant to stir our affections for Christ. More specifically, we should build habits that stimulate our affection for Jesus. We are supposed to disrupt our everyday life to do things that pull us out of the monotony, and into a deeper and more loving relationship with the Lord. The disciplines that can help us stir affections are prayer, bible study and meditation, worship both corporate and private, servanthood, stewardship, fasting, silence, and solitude. These habits should bring about a deeper intimacy with God.

I have often, in my many years of interaction with the NAR heard, "I do not want to put God in a box." I understand their meaning. They want to experience God in all His fullness with no borders or boundaries. The difficulty I have with this statement is that God has placed himself in a box so to speak. There are borders and boundaries for our worship of Him. The eternal indescribable God in heaven has placed himself into a book that describes Him in vivid detail. He has given us a way to experience Him by wrapping His son in flesh. He has made himself known to us. His word the Bible is His way of making Himself known. It is the eternal God limiting Himself to be made known to man, and to be known by man. God has confined Himself to be written about in a book. Graciously so, or we would not know Him.

We can know him and stir up our affections for Him by the means that He has given us. There are methods of worship that fall outside of Christian Orthodoxy. Those means of worship, that the NAR participates in, God has strictly forbidden. I have sought to clearly lay out those practices that the NAR engages in that God says are off limits. My opinion has been formed by research, and my own eyewitness testimony over many years. The things this movement are involved in to seek to stir their affections for Christ, only serves to stir their affections for more emotional experiences. We should take care that we do the things that God has approved for us to know Him and to experience Him. When we seek to build these few spiritual disciplines into our lives we will grow an affection for the Lord that is healthy, and mature.

When we are open emotionally to experience God in various ways that can be very good. The danger comes when we don't base that experience on an accurate knowledge of biblical truth. If emotions and experiences are more important than biblical truth, then the danger is that we might make our emotionally charged experiences our truth. Additionally, we could be opening ourselves up to other spiritual powers that are not of God. That is where biblical knowledge is so essential. Our biblical knowledge serves to authenticate the truth. When filled with the word of God our biblical discernment will aid us. This is the power that relativism occasionally holds over people. Relativism says my experience is my truth, and your experience is your truth. Relativism has created a type of idolatry, the worship or adoration of our own emotional experiences. Even as Christians we can fall prey to this type of idolatrous relativism. That is why we must balance Biblical truth with our spiritual experiences. Then our discernment will take over and warn us when something is amiss.

In closing, I urge you to carefully and prayerfully consider whether or not to allow this "Gangrenous Divergent" teaching, theology, and practice to remain in your Christ-honoring churches anymore. Church leaders and pastors, I ask you to please discern for yourselves if you should continue to use materials, visit conferences, revivals, and or support Bethel Church, Bill Johnson, the WOF, TWM, NAR or any of their associates. It can damage your faith, and/or the faith of your congregations. I have witnessed firsthand how it has caused irreversible spiritual injury. In my 20 years of youth and church ministry experience, I have observed personally how destructive it can be. In this book, I have sought to faithfully lay out the evidence, so that you can make an educated theological decision whether it is prudent to leave behind and or discontinue connection with the teaching of the WOF, TWM, NAR and Bill Johnson's Bethel Church in Redding California. My hope is that you are now able to make a well-informed, Spirit led decision. "The grace of the Lord Jesus Christ, and the love of God, and the fellowship of the Holy Spirit be with you all."[162]

---

162   *2 Corinthians 13:14 (ESV)*

CHAPTER SUMMARY

It is possible for people to navigate in the supernatural with great signs and wonders and NOT be true followers of Christ (Matthew 7:15-23; Deuteronomy 13:1-5).

There could be three possibilities why False Teachers are able to perform miracles:

1. Jesus name is just that powerful (Acts 21)

2. They are working in the supernatural power of the enemy and attributing the works of the enemy to Christ.

3. The signs and wonders are not miraculous at all

Please use your discernment when dealing with the WOF, TWM, or NAR

DIVERGENT THEOLOGY

APPENDIX I: SOURCES REFERENCED / CITED

Redding Newspaper critique
http://www.redding.com/news/bethels-signs-and-wonders-include-angel-feathers-gold-dust-and-diamonds-ep-377152155-353401081.html
https://www.youtube.com/watch?v=w3oFFZQqKdc
https://www.youtube.com/watch?v=dWeUNoR30_0
https://www.youtube.com/watch?v=2X1HC-3s3uI
https://www.youtube.com/watch?v=7fuhR7WEnrI

The Agony of Deceit
http://www.huffingtonpost.com/pastor-rick-henderson/osteen-meyer-prosperity-gospel_b_3790384.html
http://www.bible.ca/tongues-encyclopedia-pentecostal-preachers.htm

Bethel Heresies, cult behavior, and deadly activity
http://jesuscultureawakening.blogspot.de/2012/06/god-delivers-another-from-cult-of-jesus.html#.VvGbx8d07zK

Bill Johnson Critique regarding Smoke Cloud, Gold Dust, and Angel Feathers
http://www.worldviewweekend.com/tube/video/exposing-false-teaching-bill-johnson-bethel-church-redding-ca

Heretical quotes from Bill Johnson
http://www.zedekiahlist.com/cgi-bin/quotes.pl?&id=57408920

Full Critique of Bethel
http://jesuscultureawakening.blogspot.de/search/label/Bill%20Johnson#.VvG06Md07zJ

Thorough Heretical dissection of Bethel's teachings
https://shepherdguardian.wordpress.com/2013/09/05/heresy-alert-bill-johnson-jesus-culture-and-bethel-church/

Bethel TV's own Glory Cloud Video
https://www.youtube.com/watch?v=lvJMPccZR2Y

More Prosperity YouTube Channel Bethel TV
https://www.youtube.com/user/ibetheltv/videos

Schmelzer, Carsten. (Vineyard AG Theologie)
Einblicke in Bill Johnsons Heilungstheologie.
http://pastor-storch.de/wp-content/uploads/2011/09/Bill-Johnsons-Heilungstheologie.pdf (EPUB File)

Kariuki, Mumbi. *Deception In The Church*: The New Apostolic Reformation And The Emergent Church. N.p.: CreateSpace Independent Platform, 2016. Print.

Osborn, Fredrick. *The New Reformation: An Assessment of the New Apostolic Reformation from Toronto to Redding.* N.p.: Fredrick Osborn, 2015.

Geivett, R. Douglas., and Holly Pivec. *A New Apostolic Reformation?: A Biblical Response to a Worldwide Movement.* Print.

Geivett, R. Douglas., and Holly Pivec. *God's Super-apostles: Encountering the Worldwide Prophets and Apostles Movement.* Print.

McConnell, D. R. *A Different Gospel: A Historical and Biblical Analysis of the Modern Faith Movement.* Peabody, MA: Hendrickson, 1988. Print.

Ross, Christopher. *The New Apostolic Reformation: An Analysis and Critique*. 2005. Print.

Simpson, Sandy. *The New Apostolic Reformation: What Is It and Where Is It Going?* Pearl City, HI: Apologetics Coordination Team (ACT), 2004. Print.

Strom, Andrew. *Kundalini Warning: Are False Spirits Invading the Church?* United States: Revival School, 2010. Print.

Weaver, John. *The New Apostolic Reformation: History of a Modern Charismatic Movement*. Print.

DIVERGENT THEOLOGY

APPENDIX II: BILL JOHNSON QUOTES AND ASSOCIATIONS

Bill Johnson Teaches the Health Gospel
https://www.youtube.com/watch?v=UzAwFYKe3h0

Healing in the Atonement
http://youthapologeticstraining.com/bill-johnson-and-healing-in-the-atonement/

Bible Teachings about Necromancy
http://bible.knowing-jesus.com/topics/Necromancy

Bill Johnson Wolf in sheep's clothing
http://www.thebereancall.org/content/august-2012-q-and-a-1

Documentary on Lakeland Revival: and Todd Bentley Anointed by Bill Johnson as an Apostle through the NAR and Anointing service, and soon thereafter Bentley divorced his wife for "irreconcilable differences." He had had an ongoing affair with an assistant from the ministry.
https://www.youtube.com/watch?v=UDEsXVUQeLo

Todd Bentley Controversy
http://www.charismamag.com/spirit/devotionals/live-extraordinarily?view=article&id=2778:leaders-of-todd-bentleys-former-ministry-break-silence&catid=566

Bill Johnson God does not Cause Illness and never allows it either
http://www.donotbesurprised.com/2013/08/bill-johnson-god-does-not-cause-illness.html

APPENDIX II | DIVERGENT THEOLOGY

Bill Johnson explains the Gold Dust and Angel Feathers
https://www.youtube.com/watch?v=tcPkOR4Lwj0

Ben Fitzgerald the one who is seen here grave sucking at two different graves
https://www.youtube.com/watch?v=LrHPTs8cLls
http://www.awakeningeurope.com/godfest-team-en/ben-fitzgerald

Kundalini Practices:
https://en.wikipedia.org/wiki/Kundalini

Orthodox critique of Toronto Blessing
http://orthodoxinfo.com/inquirers/toronto.aspx

Smith Wigglesworth: Whom Bill Johnson Praises and reveres and Ben Fitzgerald visited his grave and sucked the Holy Spirit from his bones
https://www.youtube.com/watch?v=LrHPTs8cLls
https://en.wikipedia.org/wiki/Smith_Wigglesworth

Bill Johnson teaches on Jesus emptying himself of Divinity
http://mywordlikefire.com/2014/07/21/bethels-bill-johnson-jesus-was-so-empty-of-divine-capacity/

Bill Johnson Born Again Jesus Part 1
https://notunlikelee.wordpress.com/2010/09/17/bill-johnsons-born-again-jesus-part-i/

Bill Johnson Born Again Jesus Part 2
https://notunlikelee.wordpress.com/2010/11/07/bill-johnsons-born-again-jesus-part-ii/

Bill Johnson New Age Christ Part 1
https://notunlikelee.wordpress.com/2012/03/11/bill-johnsons-christology-a-new-age-christ/

Bill Johnson New Age Christ Part 2
https://notunlikelee.wordpress.com/2012/04/02/bill-johnsons-christology-a-new-christ-part-ii/

Bill Johnson New Age Christ Part 3
https://notunlikelee.wordpress.com/2012/04/17/bill-johnsons-christology-a-new-age-christ-part-iiia/

Bill Johnson New Age Christ Part 3b
https://notunlikelee.wordpress.com/2012/04/27/bill-johnsons-christology-a-new-age-christ-part-iiib/

Bill Johnson New Age Christ Part 4
https://notunlikelee.wordpress.com/2012/06/25/bill-johnsons-christology-a-new-age-christ-part-iv-conclusion/

Word of Faith Atonement
http://www.givingananswer.org/articles/wordoffaithatonement.html

Troubling Bill Johnson Quotes
When Heaven Invades Earth

Page 79
Christological Heresies (Adoptionism)
"The anointing is what linked Jesus, the man, to the divine, enabling him to destroy the works of the devil."

Page 80
(Anti-Trinitarianism)
"It was the Holy Spirit that revealed the Father to Jesus" (Anti-Trinitarianism)

Page 79
(Jesus Experiential Anointing? He was not already the Anointed one from birth)
"Christ is not Jesus' last name. The word Christ means the "Anointed One" or "Messiah." It is a title that points to an experience. It was not sufficient that Jesus be sent from heaven to earth with a title. He had to receive the anointing in an experience to accomplish what the father desired."

Page 29
(Jesus not divine laid aside His divinity, Denial of Pre-existent Christ and Hypostasis)
"Jesus could not heal the sick. Neither could he deliver the tormented from demons or raise the dead. To believe otherwise is to ignore what he said about Himself, and more importantly, to miss the purpose of His self-imposed restrictions to live as a man."

"Jesus Christ said of Himself, "The Son can do nothing." In the Greek language, that word nothing has a unique meaning--it means NOTH-

ING, just like it does in English! He had NO supernatural capabilities whatsoever! While he is 100 Percent God, He chose to live with the same limitations that man would face once he was redeemed. He made that point over and over again. Jesus became the model for all who would embrace the invitation to invade the impossible in His name. He performed miracles, wonders, and signs, as a man in right relationship to God … not as God. If he performed miracles because he was God, then they would be unattainable for us. But if He did them as a man, I am responsible to pursue His lifestyle. Recapturing the simple truth changes everything … and makes possible a full restoration of the ministry of Jesus in His church."

Page 27
(Miracles depend on us and our desperation?)
"The lack of miracles isn't because it is not in God's will for us. The problem exists between our ears. As a result, a transformation—a renewing of the mind—is needed, and it's only possible through a work of the Holy Spirit that typically comes upon desperate people."Page 27
(The Gospel up to this point has not been authentic?)
"Stories of this nature are becoming the norm (i.e. miracles), and the company of people who have joined this quest for an authentic gospel—the gospel of the Kingdom—is increasing. Loving God and His people is an honor."

Dominionism:
Page 30
"Man was created in the image of God and placed in the Father's ultimate expression of beauty and peace: The Garden of Eden. Outside of that Garden, it was a different story. It was without the order and blessing contained within and was in great need of the touch of God's delegated one—Adam … But in Genesis chapter 1 we discover it's not a perfect universe. Satan had rebelled and had been cast out of Heaven,

and with him, a portion of the fallen angels took dominion of the earth. It's obvious why the rest of the planet needed to be subdued—it was under the influence of darkness (Genesis 1:2). God could have destroyed the devil and his host with a word, but instead, He chose to defeat darkness through His delegated authority—those made in His image who were lovers of God by choice."

Page 31
"This highest of honors (Dominion over the earth) was chosen because love always chooses the best. That is the beginning of the romance of our creation … created in His image, for intimacy, that dominion might be expressed through love. It is from this revelation that we are to learn to walk as His ambassadors, thus defeating the "Prince of this world." The stage was set for all of darkness to fall as man exercised His godly influence over creation. But instead, man fell."

"Satan didn't come into the Garden of Eden violently and take possession of Adam and Eve. He couldn't! Why? He had no dominion there. Dominion empowers. And since man was given the keys of the dominion over the planet, the devil would have to get his authority from them. The suggestion to eat the forbidden fruit was simply the devil's effort to get Adam and Eve to agree with him in opposition to God, thus empowering him. Through that agreement, he is enabled to kill, steal, and destroy. It's important to realize that even today, Satan is empowered through man's agreement."

"Mankind's authority to rule was forfeited when Adam ate the forbidden fruit. Paul said, "You are that one's slaves whom you obey." In that one act, mankind became the slave and possession of the Evil One. All that Adam owned, including the title deed to the planet with its corresponding position of rule, became part of the devil's spoil. God's predetermined plan of redemption immediately kicked into play, "I will put enmity between you and the woman, and between your seed and her seed; He shall bruise your head, and you shall bruise His heel." Jesus would come to reclaim all that was lost."

Richard's thoughts on Dominionism
If Jesus died on the cross to restore Dominion back to man, then why don't we have it? We have forgiveness of sins, right? We have Penal Substitution, right? If Dominion was what Jesus restored, then we should not have to do anything to receive it, it would also be a gift of the grace of God just as the remission of sins is received by grace through faith!

Page 31
(Dominionism: Atonement view)
"God's plan of rulership for man never ceased. Jesus came to bear man's penalty for sin and recapture what had been lost. Luke 19:10 says that Jesus came "to seek and to save that which was lost." Not only was mankind lost to sin, his dominion over planet earth was also lost. Jesus came to recapture both."
Chapter two "Commission Restored" in *When Heaven Invades Earth* is a Manifesto on Dominionism. Almost every single section describes Dominionism from the Garden to the Cross.

Page 34

In *When Heaven Invades Earth* … Johnson says, "We are so entrenched in unbelief that anything contrary to this worldview is thought to be of the devil. So it is with the idea of the church having a dominating impact before Jesus returns. It's almost as though we want to defend the right to be small in number and make it by the skin of our teeth. Embracing a belief system that requires no faith is dangerous. It is contrary to the nature of God and all that the Scriptures declare. Since He plans to do above all we could ask or think, according to Ephesians 3:20, His promises by nature challenge our intellect and expectations. "(Jerusalem) did not consider her destiny; therefore her collapse was awesome." (Lamentations 1:9) The result of forgetting His promises is not one we can afford."

Richard's thoughts about the above quote
In this passage, Johnson seems to be saying that if we like Jerusalem forget our "destiny," then our collapse will, like Jerusalem, be awesome. I wondered where this translation came from. I compared all English translations and the word "destiny" did not appear in any of them. I do not know which translation he uses, but it does not appear in any English versions that I found. The Hebrew word אחרית (Pronounced 'achariyth') has the connotation of, "the last or end, hence the future; also posterity: — (last, latter) end (time), hinder (utter) -most, length, posterity, remnant, residue, or reward." It is relatively obvious after following the NAR and WOF movement for many years that they love this word. They are seeking to get everyone living "in their destiny," and for the NAR, that "destiny" means having dominion, health, wealth and prosperity. Christian victory has historically been voctory over sin, but Christian victory for the NAR is living in their "destiny."

Page 37
"Most Christians repent enough to get forgiven, but not enough to see the kingdom."

Page 38
"Repentance is not complete until it envisions His kingdom."

Gnosticism
Page 39
"Our abundant life is hidden in the kingdom realm. And only faith can make the withdrawals."

Kingdom Now or Dominionism

Page 39
"The Christian life has been harnessed to this goal, verbalized in the Lord's Model Prayer: "Your kingdom come. Your will be done on earth as it is in heaven." His dominion is realized when what happens here is as it is in heaven."

Page 42
"While he (a man who was a burn victim and lived with numbness) was still talking I began to pray for him with my hand on his shoulder. I had to do so quickly. I had become aware of the Kingdom were no numbness existed."

Page 45
"The invisible realm is superior to the natural. The reality of that invisible world dominates the natural world we live … both positively and negatively."

"For example, if I believe that God allows sickness in order to build character, I'll not have confidence praying in most situations where healing is needed. But, if I believe that sickness is to the body what sin is to the soul, then no disease will intimidate me."

Page 46
"I can acknowledge the existence of the tumor and still have faith in the provision of His stripes for my healing … I was provisionally healed 2000 years ago. It is the product of the kingdom of Heaven--a superior reality. There are no tumors in heaven, and faith brings that reality into this one."

"Would Satan like to inflict heaven with cancer? Of course, he would. But he has no dominion there. He only has dominion here when and where man has come into agreement."

Page 47
"Through faith, man is able to come into agreement with the mind of God."

Page 47
"The Holy Spirit lives in my spirit. That is the place of communion with God. As we learn to receive from our spirits, we learn how to be Spirit-led."

Page 68
"Jesus was sleeping in the middle of a life-threatening storm. The disciples woke him because they were afraid of dying. He exercised authority and released peace over the storm. It was the peace of Heaven that enabled him to sleep. And it was that same peace that subdued the storm. You only have authority over the storm you can sleep in."

Works Salvation
Page 72:
"He'll give us His baptism of fire if we'll give him something burning."
"Contentment short of God's purposes would mean having to learn to live with the enemy. That is what it is like when a believer is baptized in the Holy Spirit but never goes beyond speaking in tongues. When we become satisfied apart from God's ultimate purpose of dominion, we learn to tolerate the devil in some area of our life."
"Some have put it this way: one baptism, many fillings. Why? We leak."

Page 74
"Part of the privilege of ministry is learning how to release the Holy Spirit in a location."
"Many opportunities for ministry have developed as I've learned how to release his presence in the marketplace."

Page 75
"The anointing is substance. It is the actual presence of the Holy Spirit, and He can be released into our surroundings."

Special Revelation
Page 76:
"None of us has a full grasp of scripture, but we all have the Holy Spirit. He is our common denominator who will always lead us into truth. But to follow him, we must be willing to follow off the map—to go beyond what we know. To do so successfully, we must recognize his presence above all."

Richard's thoughts about Jesus being Baptized in the Holy Spirit
Was Jesus Baptized in the Holy Spirit? No, He is the second person of the Godhead, and never stopped being the Son of God, and was eternally connected to the Godhead in perfect unity. Thus, He does not need to be baptized in the Holy Spirit or get direction or explanation of who the Father is from the Holy Spirit.
"He (Jesus) illustrated this lifestyle after his Holy Spirit baptism. He followed the Holy Spirits leading, even when it seemed unreasonable, which it often did."

Page 80
On page 80, According to Johnson, Exodus 40:15 describes the Holy Ghost anointing and that it was a qualification for service as a priest in the Old Testament. This passage here describes the sons of Aaron being anointed and consecrated as priests. Levitical lineage was the qualification for priesthood, not a Holy Ghost anointing. In Exodus 40 the sons of Aaron were being anointed with oil and consecrated for the work of their new position. This is terrible exegesis and a complete lack of understanding of the Old Testament and its economy.

"So revered is the Holy Spirit in the Godhead, that Jesus said, "anyone who speaks a word against the Son of Man, it will be forgiven him; but whoever speaks against the Holy Spirit, it will not be forgiven him, either in this age or in the age to come."

This passage that Johnson is referring to, is actually talking about the "blasphemy of the Holy Spirit" or what has been understood for ages in Christian history as the continual hardening of heart to the extension of grace to the unbeliever. This passage is not about how the Holy Spirit is the most revered person in the Godhead.

Page 81
"The spirit of the antichrist is at work today, attempting to influence believers to reject everything that has to do with the Holy Spirit's anointing ... That spirit (Johnson is describing the Spirit of religion and the Anti-Christ) feeds on the residue of past revivals."

Page 83-84
"If our study of the Bible doesn't lead us to a deeper relationship (an encounter), with God, then it simply is adding to our tendency towards spiritual pride. We increase our knowledge of the Bible to feel good about our standing with God, and to better equip us to argue with those who disagree with us ... Jesus did not say, "My sheep will know my book." It is his voice that we are to know."

How are we as Christians to recognize the voice of the Savior? If we know His word, we know His voice. Jesus Himself said that the scriptures prophesy about Him and He also prayed in John 17:17 "Sanctify them in the truth; your word is truth!"

Page 84
"The antichrist spirit has a goal for the Church—embrace Jesus apart from the anointing. Without the anointing, He becomes a safe religious figure who is sure not to challenge or offend us."

Page 88
"My Promise meant that I would make the outpouring of the Holy Spirit, with the full manifestations of His gifts—the sole purpose for my existence. And I would never stray from that call—no matter what! He touched me, and I have pursued without fail."

Page 90
Admission of the New Apostolic order that Johnson is a part of
"But now this gravitational pull toward fathers is happening even within denominations. Such a gathering of believers allows for differences in nonessential doctrines without causing division. Many consider this movement to be a restoration of the *apostolic* (emphasis added) order of God."

Page 93
Special Revelation & removing power from the Word of God
"But in reality, the Bible is a closed book. Anything I can get from the Word without God will not change my life. It is closed to ensure that I remain dependent on the Holy Spirit … He loves to feed those who are truly hungry."

Page 93
Historical Exegesis is not the right way to understand the Bible
"When I treat the Bible as a road map, I live as though I can find my way through my own understanding of His book. I believe this perspective of scriptures actually describes living under the law, not living under grace."

Page 94
"The doctrine (Cessationism) stating signs and wonders are no longer needed because we have the Bible (this is actually not the correct view of Cessationism) was created by people who hadn't seen God's power and needed an explanation to justify their own powerless churches."

Richard's comments
This is a grave accusation. Johnson has to somehow give evidence that this was the case in the development of the view of Cessationism. Johnson prides himself on ecumenicalism, and it is hard to see how these accusations could be creating unity.

Page 94
"Unless Scripture leads me to Him, I only become better equipped to debate with those who disagree with my way of thinking."

Richard's comments
Johnson seems to be forgetting all the superior reasons for reading, studying, and meditating on scripture beside winning debates. For instance, the following verses give us enough reasons for studying, meditating on, and committing the Bible to memory.

Psalm 119:9
How can a young man keep his way pure? By guarding it according to your word. *(To seek purity)*

Psalm 119:11
I have stored up your word in my heart, that I might not sin against you. *(To resist sin)*

Psalm 119:16
I will delight in your statutes; I will not forget your word *(For our delight in the Lord)*

Psalm 119:28
My soul melts away for sorrow; strengthen me according to your word! *(To strengthen our souls)*

Psalm 119:67
Before I was afflicted I went astray, but now I keep your word. *(To keep us from wandering and to help us return to the Lord when we stray)*

Psalm 119:81
My soul longs for your salvation; I hope in your word. *(For our salvation and others)*

Psalm 119:105
Your word is a lamp to my feet and a light to my path. *(For guidance)*

Psalm 119:169
Let my cry come before you, O Lord; give me understanding according to your word! *(For understanding)*

Psalm 119:170
Let my plea come before you; deliver me according to your word. *(For deliverance)*

Psalm 119:172
My tongue will sing of your word, for all your commandments are right. *(To know His righteousness and commands)*

APPENDIX II | DIVERGENT THEOLOGY

John 2:22
When therefore he was raised from the dead, his disciples remembered that he had said this, and they believed the Scripture and the word that Jesus had spoken. *(To embolden and receive belief)*

John 5:39-40
You search the Scriptures because you think that in them you have eternal life; and it is they that bear witness about me, yet you refuse to come to me that you may have life. *(To know Jesus)*

John 17:17
"Sanctify them in the truth; your word is truth." *(For our sanctification)*

1 Timothy 4:13
Until I come, devote yourself to the public reading of Scripture, to exhortation, to teaching. *(For exhortation and teaching)*

2 Timothy 3:16
All Scripture is breathed out by God and profitable for teaching, for reproof, for correction, and for training in righteousness. *(For our correction & righteousness)*

Richard's comments
These are just a few scriptures that show us what they are useful for. Johnson seems to put more emphasis on experience than the Bible. He sees the Bible at best as a supplement or complement to those experiences, and at worst could be teaching that the word of God might be a hindrance in your spiritual life. In so doing, he seriously diminishes the word of God in relation to our Christian life.

Page 103
"Pursue the men and women of God who carry an anointing in their lives for the miraculous. Such an anointing can be transferred to others through the laying on of hands."

Richard's comments
Peter, in Acts 8:9-24 condemns Simon the magician for asking to pay for this type of power, but Johnson encourages believers to pursue people who will transfer those types of powers.

Page 108
"Christlike character can never be fully developed without serving under the anointing." (in other words a ministry like his or another NAR leader)

Page 110
"Doesn't it seem strange that our whole Christian life should be focused on overcoming something that has already been defeated? Sin and its nature have been yanked out by the roots."

Richard's comments
This sounds suspiciously like he means we have no more sin nature which is the heresy called Pelagianism (refer to Appendix III Heresies). The question then arises, have we become sinlessly perfect? And the answer is a resounding NO!

Page 113
Johnson described a situation when he encountered God "coursing through" his body like being electrocuted. Does the Holy Spirit do this course through people's bodies like electricity?

Richard's comments

Johnson's footnotes on page 113 explain that praying for resurrection would be appropriate when healing has not happened. Why would you pray for resurrection at the point when believers die? One could get the impression as you read that Johnson's best heaven is actually here on earth.

Page 116
Johnson on page 116 shows how he is not open to criticism. He says he will not read books or work that criticizes the Toronto blessing.

Page 116
"for decades the church has been guilty of creating doctrine to justify their lack of power, instead of crying out to God until he changes them. The lie they came to believe is giving rise to an entire branch of theology that has infected the body of Christ with a fear of the Holy Spirit."

Page 117
On page 117, Johnson prays for brain diseases, for instance, the healing of dyslexia and other brain diseases. Dyslexia is a learning disorder, not a disease. Is he then going to pray for learning disorders and other genetic disabilities too? This type of "healing" gives rise to the question, "is Down Syndrome meant to be healed?" Like I have heard many times before, "Do you have faith that Ana your daughter will be healed of Down Syndrome?"

Page 119
At the beginning of chapter 11, Johnson quotes the Moravian missionaries who were setting off to the West Indies. He quotes them as saying, "Win for the lamb that was slain the reward for his suffering." With a little research, Johnson would have been able to find out that this is not how that quote reads. The quote actually reads, "May the lamb that

was slain receive the reward of his suffering." It may be just semantics, but these few words make a huge difference. In Johnson's view, we help the Lamb (Jesus) win the reward for suffering through Dominionism. But in the quote from John Leonard Dober and David Nitschmann, the Moravian missionaries from Herrnhut, Germany, the quote reads much differently. These Moravian missionaries viewed their service as necessary for Christ to receive the reward for His suffering. On the other hand, Johnson describes all the way through his book how we take an active role in the Atonement of Christ.

https://en.wikipedia.org/wiki/Moravian_slaves

http://www.desiringgod.org/messages/at-the-price-of-gods-own-blood

Page 122

On this page, Johnson lays out his Dominionism theology for cities. Johnson gives Bethsaida and Chorazin as examples. He said that that there had to be some measure of faith in those cities for Jesus to have done any miracles at all. This is horrific exegesis. The passage never once intimates that they had faith, rather Jesus is leveling a harsh rebuke that has nothing to do with whether the miracles that were performed were because of some semblance of faith and that is why they were done. He made a huge jump to interpret the passage that way and then makes a huge jump into his Dominionism theology for cities. Johnson commits rather flagrant eisegesis, which is the process of interpreting a text or portion of text in such a way that the reader introduces his or her own presuppositions, agendas into the text. This process is also known as proof-texting where a reader believes some form of theology and goes to search out a text that might confirm the said theology or belief.

Page 124

"Jesus again looked to see what the Father was doing and now noticed that He was turning water into wine. So Jesus followed His lead and did the miracle. Her (Mary's) faith so touched the heart of the Father that he apparently changed the chosen time to unveil Jesus as the miracle worker. Faith moves heaven so that heaven will move earth."

Page 126
"Without miracles, there can *never* (emphasis added) be a full revelation of Jesus."

Page 127
"Miracles provide the grace for repentance."

Page 127
"It wasn't a complete message without a demonstration of the power of God. It's how God says amen to his own declared word!"

Richard's comments
From this and other explanations in this book, it would seem that Johnson believes that whenever no miracle takes place alongside gospel proclamation, the message is incomplete.

Page 129
Johnson says people are deceived who use means, like Bible study, and other Christian religious traditions to understand God, but not signs.
"We've gone as far as we can with our present understanding of scripture. It's time to let signs have their place."

Page 136
"When we minister in the anointing, we actually give away the presence of God—we impart him to others ... He has made us stewards of the presence of God."

"He looks for those who are willing to be smeared with Him, allowing His presence to affect others for good."

Page 137
"Getting us to heaven is not near as great a challenge as it is to get heaven into us."

Page 138
Johnson describes "Gate Churches" that "steward" the heavenly realm for an entire city.

His wife Beni in her writings also talks about "thin places" where the distance between heaven and earth is thin and heaven is breaking through the natural realm in tangible ways. These places include Redding, CA, Toronto, Lakeland, FL, and Kansas City, MO.

Page 139
"I believe angels have been bored because we live the kind of lifestyle that doesn't require much of their help."

Richard's comments
Does Johnson mean that Angels that stand in the presence of the Holy God are bored? This is outrageous. They stand before the throne for all eternity singing, "Holy, Holy, Holy is the Lord God almighty who was, and is, and is to come." They are by no means bored by any duty that the Lord appoints them to do.

Page 140
"As such I contain a gate to heaven, with a ladder providing angelic activities according to the need of the moment. Simply put, I am an open heaven!"

"I believe angels pick up the fragrance of the throne room through the word spoken by people."

APPENDIX II | DIVERGENT THEOLOGY

"They (angels) can tell when a word has its origins in the heart of the father. And, in turn they recognize that word as their assignment."

Page 149
"Doesn't it honor Him more when we think of ourselves as free from sin because He said we are?"

Page 154
"I honestly believe Satan will allow his strategies to become known so that we will react accordingly."

Page 159
"Many church historians have declared this revival to be genuine."
Johnson does not name one single "church historian" that has "declared" this to be a genuine revival. He cannot make such a claim without reference and resource. He cannot claim, "because I said so" as a reference.

"They (Again who is he referring to here?) have seen that it bears the same fruit, and causes the same stirrings in the church, as previous revivals in history. It's been encouraging to hear various theologians (more nameless theologians) affirming this revival as a true move of God. Yet it's not their seal of approval I look for."

Page 179
"I pay no attention to the warnings of possible excess (in regards to signs and wonders) from those who are satisfied with lack."
"Jesus intends for us to be mature before he returns."

Page 182
"The exploits of the present and coming revival will surpass all the accomplishments of the church in all history combined. Over 1 Billion souls will be saved. Stadiums will be filled with people 24 hours a day,

for days on end, with miracles beyond number: healings, conversions, resurrections and deliverances too many to count. No special speaker, no well-known miracle worker, just the church being what God has called her to be. And all this will be the outgrowth of the unity of faith."

Page 183
"The entire church will receive a fresh revelation of Jesus Christ especially through that book (referring to the Book of Revelation). This (The Book of Revelation) that has been so mysterious will be understood."

Page 183
"The coming increase in Revelation of Jesus will be measurable through new dimensions of worship—corporate throne room experiences."

Page 187
"As wonderful as our spiritual roots are, they are insufficient. What was good for yesterday is deficient for today. To insist that we stay with what our fathers fought for is to insult our forefathers."
"There is very little of what we know as church life that will remain untouched in the next 10 years."

The Supernatural Power of a Transformed Mind

Dominionism
Page 31
"Of course, we know that the original plan got derailed, and that Adam forfeited the rulership God gave him over the earth, putting humanity into slavery to the enemy … When that prophecy was fulfilled in the death and resurrection of Jesus Christ, God took back the authority man had given away and reclaimed our purpose on this earth. He gave us a clear field to run toward the original goal—and run with all our might. We, the Church, are called to extend His rule in this earthly

sphere, just as Adam was called to do. We see this in each commission shown in the gospel: the commission of the 12, the commission of the 70 and the 72, and the Great Commission. God gave the same instructions: In essence, "Go heal the sick, preach the good news, demonstrate who I am and what I am like. Extend My Kingdom!"

Page 37

"Renewing the mind begins with repentance. That is the gateway to return to our original assignment on earth. Jesus said, "Repent, for the kingdom of heaven is at hand." Too many Christians, repent refers to having an altar call for people to come forward and at the altar and we get right with God. That is a legitimate expression of repentance, but it's not what the word repentance means. "Re" means to go back. "Pent" is like the penthouse, the top floor of the building. Repent, then, means to go back to God's perspective on reality. And in that perspective there is a renewal, a reformation that affects our intellect, our emotions, and every part of our lives."

Page 75-76

"Christians are absolutely responsible for bringing divine healing to people, "proving the will of God," bringing earthly reality into line with what's true in heaven. Healing is part of the normal Christian life. God put it in his book; He illustrated it in the life of Jesus. He told us to emulate what Jesus did. So why is it so easy for us to be fully convinced when we pray for someone to be saved that our prayer will work, and yet when we pray for healing we find it difficult to believe they will be healed? Because salvation, as it pertains to a born-again experience, has been embraced and taught continuously by the Church for centuries, the revelation of healing has not been widely embraced, and has even been fought. Today in many Churches, if you pray for people to be healed you are considered to be working under the influence of the devil, while disease is considered a gift from God to make people better Christians!

Think about how badly the church has backslidden, to believe such lies! We have tolerated the deception that accuses God of doing evil, which is why today healing remains so controversial, little-practiced and little-understood."

"Revelation is not something you can dig out of a Theological book or study guide. It's not even something you can unravel in the Bible all by yourself."

The Supernatural Power of a Transformed Mind (Study Guide)
(Sample Page 1 Introduction)
"What is free to operate in Heaven—joy, peace, wisdom, health, wholeness, and all the other good promises we read about in the Bible—should be free to operate here on the planet … What is not free to operate there—sickness, disease, spiritual bondage, and sin—should not be free to operate here, period."

(Sample Page 2 Day 1)
"Has it ever occurred to you that one of your jobs on earth is … to prove the will of God? Your calling and my calling as believers may be too massive to fully understand, but the Bible's command is clear: Our job is to demonstrate that the reality that exists in Heaven can be manifested right here, right now. We are not just to be people who believe the right things about God, but people who put the will of God on display, expressing it and causing others to realize, "oh so that's what God is like." … Jesus taught and demonstrated that the Kingdom of God is a present tense reality—it exists now in the invisible realm and is superior to everything in the visible realm."

(Sample Page 3 Day 2)
Quotes from *The Supernatural Power of a Transformed Mind: Access to a Life of Miracles* Page 31, 35, 41

This is, of course, a total misinterpretation of Romans 12:1-2. The word there for prove is "dokimadzo," and it means to test by implication to approve: allow or discern, or examine, prove, or try. This passage is saying that through nonconformity to this world, and by renewing your mind through the Scriptures, you will be able to know the will of God, test it and approve what He wants you to do. This is, of course, poor exegesis and hermeneutics.

Explanation of Dominionism: Adam and Eve lost Dominion of the earth to Satan. The Resurrected Christ appointed the church to regain dominion of all the earth. Christ either cannot or will not return until the Church has accomplished this.

(Sample Page 4 Day 3)
"God's idea was to have a planet engulfed in His glorious rule, with mankind flawlessly "proving the will of God" on earth as it is in Heaven … Of course, we know the original plan got derailed, and that Adam forfeited the rulership God gave him over the earth, putting humanity into slavery to the enemy … In the death and resurrection of Jesus Christ, God took back the authority man had given away and reclaimed our purpose on this earth … We, the Church, are called to extend His rule in this earthly sphere, just as Adam was called to do."

Has the Church regained and reclaimed Rulership? Dominion? Authority?

"Hosting the Presence" is the belief that our divine assignment is to be carriers of the presence of God
"Jesus models, better than anyone in Scripture, how to host the presence of the Lord. I would remind you that, obviously, Jesus is God. He is eternal. He is not a created being but he emptied himself and became a man and learned how to host the presence of the Lord. Jesus himself said that

he set aside his divinity. The Scriptures tell us that he emptied himself. He could do nothing of himself. None of the miracles did he do as God. He did them all as a man, yielded to God. They are all expressions of a life under the influence of the Holy Spirit. Jesus learned to host the presence of the Lord and in doing so was so conscious of God upon him that when a woman touched his clothing he could tell power had been released from him."

"Imagine being so aware of the Spirit of God on you that, even though you have conversations going on with people around you, even though there is a crowd pushing in around you and touching you, when one person that touches you in faith and there is a withdrawal from your account of presence, or power, you are so conscious of what you are carrying that you realize presence has been released through you. It wasn't because the presence in him was depleted, because the Spirit of God was given to him without measure. It was just that he could tell that there had been a demand put upon what he carried."

Manifesto for a Normal Christian Life (Sample Kindle Edition)
"And you will always reflect the nature of the world we are most aware of. What you live conscious of is what you will reproduce in the world around you."

Manifesto for a Normal Christian Life (Sample Kindle Edition)
"The Holy Spirit *upon* (emphasis added) Jesus was the very power which would emanate from him to change and transform people's lives and circumstances. Torments that were on people were broken off, Diseases were healed, and hope was given to people who had no hope. Jesus ruined every funeral that he attended – including his own."

Manifesto for a Normal Christian Life (Sample Kindle Edition)
Jesus Culture is the movement that sprung out of Bethel's youth min-

istry. At a Jesus Culture Conference in Cleveland a participant claimed that she raised a baby from the dead because she "rebuked the spirit of death" in the child https://www.youtube.com/watch?v=z4HwXwqgf1s (accessed April 2017)

"They realized that Paul could not go everywhere so they would just take articles of his clothing and take them to a sick or dying or tormented person and they would be set free. It wasn't simply an act of faith. That would be noble enough in itself. But it was because the Spirit of God can actually saturate cloth. And just the simple residue, the crumbs from the table, was enough to bring deliverance and healing when it was taken from the presence of the Lord."

Manifesto for a Normal Christian Life (Sample Kindle Edition)
"I don't know how to learn anything but by experimenting. Those people who like to get it right the first time should stay away from the gifts of the Spirit, because we have to learn by experiment, in a context of safety."

Manifesto for a Normal Christian Life (Sample Kindle Edition)
"When I became conscious of the presence I would walk into the store and then I would start buying whatever I needed. And if what I wanted was in one particular place in the shop I'd walk up and down the other aisles first. I wouldn't go straight to it. I'd walk up and down the aisles, because I felt like I was a sprinkler system walking up and down, watering the entire place with presence."

Manifesto for a Normal Christian Life (Sample Kindle Edition)
"I was in too much pain to talk. I remember thinking, I'm sure glad I gave my life *back* (emphasis added) to God four days ago. I have no fear of death because I know spiritually I'm ready to meet God. I also remember thinking, how different this would all be if I were still back-

slidden. To come so close to death and not be right with God would be a scary thing."

The Essential Guide to Healing (Sample Kindle Edition)
Tells his story of His grandmother visiting heaven two times in an out of body experience. (heaven tourism/visitation)

Bill Johnson has a heretical Kenosis view of Christ
Johnson teaches that Christ set aside His deity during His earthly sojourn. Johnson has said, "Jesus was God. Eternally God. That never changed. But He chose to live with self-imposed restrictions while living on earth in the flesh—as a man. In doing so, He defeated sin, temptation, and the powers of darkness as a man. We inherit His victory—it was for us. He never sinned!" (Bill Johnson, Facebook 3/21/2011).

Consequently, that's not all that he's taught or all that his followers have said. Speaking of Jesus, Johnson wrote, "He performed miracles, wonders, and signs, as a man in right relationship to God … not as God. If He performed miracles because He was God, then they would be unattainable for us" (Johnson, *When Heaven Invades Earth*, p. 29). That's human reasoning, and by implication opens the way for a deification of man.

Johnson's view of our Lord's "emptying Himself," of which the literal meaning is "humbled himself" (Philippians 2:7), aligns very well with the Latter Rain/Word of Faith "little gods" teaching of Kenneth Copeland and others. Johnson has gone on to say, "God gave every believer the power to heal as Jesus did" (Johnson, "You've Got the Power," Charisma Online, March 2012). In line with Word of Faith teaching, Johnson and his followers speak of these apparent abilities in a way that sounds very much like mind over matter/psychic powers and departs from Scripture.

Critique of Bill Johnson's view of Penal Substitution: Jesus paid for your health on the cross.
http://www.donotbesurprised.com/2013/08/bill-johnson-god-does-not-cause-illness.html

Bethel's Healing meditation school
http://bethelsozo.com

Bill Johnson auf Deutsch
https://www.youtube.com/watch?v=2c6kyfXzhG0

John Crowder is a purveyor of the "Drunken Glory" movement and has been endorsed by Johnson on his Twitter feed
https://www.youtube.com/watch?v=mNGPA6Idopg

Todd Bentley Documentary: "Lakeland: The Movie (Documentary film on Todd Bentley & the Florida Outpouring)"
https://www.youtube.com/watch?v=UDEsXVUQeLo

Rick Joyner's Morningstar Ministries has regular interaction and partnership with Johnson
Encyclopedia of WOF Teachers
http://www.bible.ca/tongues-encyclopedia-pentecostal-preachers.htm

APPENDIX III: HERESIES

These few passages describe how we are to treat heresies. They give us a basis for naming and exposing heresies.

1 Timothy 4:1-2
2 Timothy 4:3-5
2 Timothy 3:12

"The term "heresy" refers to a false doctrine, i.e. one that is simply not true, and that is, in addition, so important that those who believe it, whom the church calls heretics, must be considered to have abandoned the faith." (Brown, Harold O. J. *Heresies: The Image of Christ in the Mirror of Heresy and Orthodoxy from the Apostles to the Present* (Garden City: Doubleday, 1984), 1.)

Theological heresies that the Third Wave Movement, Word of Faith, or New Apostolic Reformation encourages include …

Modalism: God takes different modes in different ages. According to many WOF, NAR, and TWM teachers, this is the age of the Spirit

Gnosticism: (buying and selling of spiritual offices) Blend of self-worship and philosophy. Overvaluing of knowledge with respect to faith. "The Gnostic position asserts that over and above the simple Gospel, which is all that the ordinary spirits can understand, there is a secret, higher knowledge reserved for an elite. It is natural enough for people to ask more questions that the Gospel answers; the gnostic movement attempted to give the answers, and it did so by drawing on religious sources alien to Christianity and amalgamating them with elements of the Gospel faith."

Docetism: That Christ was not truly human or only "appeared to be human" (Jesus had to be born again e.g. Joyce Meyer, Kenneth Copeland) Hypostatic Union: Kenneth Copeland teaches against the Hypostatic union that was affirmed in the Nicene Creed but largely rejected by Word of Faith (WOF) teachers

Extra Biblical Revelation: Revelation outside of or in opposition to God's word

Adoptionism: Jesus became God after He was "filled or Baptized by the Spirit"

Apollinarianism: is a view proposed by Apollinaris of Loadicea in the 4th century. He denied the humanity of Christ. Not many NAR, TWM, or NAR leaders purport this view. They usually go in the other direction to say Jesus was completely man. For instance, Bill Johnson teaches that Jesus was only a man dependent on God.

Arianism: teaches that Jesus was not divine but later became divine after His Baptism, and taught by Bill Johnson, Bethel, and other Word of Faith leaders.

Atonement: problematic views that Jesus died for our health, wealth, and prosperity, not just our sins.

Psilanthropism: Rejects Jesus divinity, either saying He never became divine, never was divine or was not pre-incarnate. All of which are in some way taught by the Third Wave Movement, Word of Faith, or New Apostolic Reformation

Antinomianism: freed by grace from any adherence to a Moral Law taught by the likes of Joyce Meyer and Joel Osteen. Never talking about sin or any dealing with a moral law.

Dominionism: Adam and Eve lost Dominion of the earth to Satan. The Resurrected Christ appointed the Church to regain dominion of all the earth. Christ either cannot or will not return until the Church has accomplished this task of taking dominion of all the earth.

Pelagianism: was proposed by British monk Pelagius who taught that original sin did not taint humanity. He taught that the will of man is still able to choose good without divine intervention. Whether Pelagius taught all facets of what is known as Pelagianism or not, it has come to be known as the teaching that says man can earn his salvation through his own effort.

John Piper on the Prosperity Gospel:
https://www.youtube.com/watch?v=G-V_91c5ojU

Matt Chandler on the Prosperity Gospel:
https://www.youtube.com/watch?v=w3oFFZQqKdc

List of Christian Heresies
https://en.wikipedia.org/wiki/List_of_Christian_heresies

Heresy Alert Bill Johnson and Jesus Culture
https://shepherdguardian.wordpress.com/2013/09/05/heresy-alert-bill-johnson-jesus-culture-and-bethel-church/

DIVERGENT THEOLOGY

APPENDIX IV: SCRIPTURE REFERENCES

"So that we may no longer be children, tossed to and fro by the waves and carried about by every wind of doctrine, by human cunning, by craftiness in deceitful schemes." — Eph.4:14 (ESV)

"This charge I entrust to you, Timothy, my child, in accordance with the prophecies previously made about you, that by them you may wage the good warfare, holding faith and a good conscience. By rejecting this, some have made shipwreck of their faith, among whom are Hymenaeus and Alexander, whom I have handed over to Satan that they may learn not to blaspheme." — 1 Timothy 1:18-20 (ESV)

"But avoid irreverent babble, for it will lead people into more and more ungodliness, and their talk will spread like gangrene. Among them are Hymenaeus and Philetus, who have swerved from the truth, saying that the resurrection has already happened. They are upsetting the faith of some." — 2 Timothy 2:16-18 (ESV)

"For there are many who are insubordinate, empty talkers and deceivers, especially those of the circumcision party. They must be silenced, since they are upsetting whole families by teaching for shameful gain what they ought not to teach." — Titus 1:10-11 (ESV)

"Do not be led away by diverse and strange teachings, for it is good for the heart to be strengthened by grace, not by foods, which have not benefited those devoted to them." — Hebrews 13:9 (ESV)

"You therefore, beloved, knowing this beforehand, take care that you are not carried away with the error of lawless people and lose your own stability." — 2 Peter 3:17 (ESV)

"I appeal to you, brothers, to watch out for those who cause divisions and create obstacles contrary to the doctrine that you have been taught; avoid them. For such persons do not serve our Lord Christ, but their own appetites, and by smooth talk and flattery they deceive the hearts of the naive." — Romans 16:17-18 (ESV)

"As I urged you when I was going to Macedonia, remain at Ephesus so that you may charge certain persons not to teach any different doctrine, nor to devote themselves to myths and endless genealogies, which promote speculations rather than the stewardship from God that is by faith." — 1 Timothy 1:3-4 (ESV)

"But even if we or an angel from heaven should preach to you a gospel contrary to the one we preached to you, let him be accursed. As we have said before, so now I say again: If anyone is preaching to you a gospel contrary to the one you received, let him be accursed." — Galatians 1:8-9 (ESV)

"But false prophets also arose among the people, just as there will be false teachers among you, who will secretly bring in destructive heresies, even denying the Master who bought them, bringing upon themselves swift destruction. And many will follow their sensuality, and because of them the way of truth will be blasphemed. And in their greed they will exploit you with false words. Their condemnation from long ago is not idle, and their destruction is not asleep." — 2 Peter 2:1-3 (ESV)

"If anyone teaches a different doctrine and does not agree with the sound words of our Lord Jesus Christ and the teaching that accords with godliness, he is puffed up with conceit and understands nothing. He has an unhealthy craving for controversy and for quarrels about words, which produce envy, dissension, slander, evil suspicions, and constant friction among people who are depraved in mind and deprived of the truth, imagining that godliness is a means of gain. But godliness with contentment is great gain, for we brought nothing into the world, and we cannot take anything out of the world. But if we have food and clothing, with these we will be content. But those who desire to be rich fall into temptation, into a snare, into many senseless and harmful desires that plunge people into ruin and destruction. For the love of money is a root of all kinds of evils. It is through this craving that some have wandered away from the faith and pierced themselves with many pangs." — 1 Timothy 6:3-10 (ESV)

Increase in false teachings in Christianity.

"For the time is coming when people will not endure sound teaching, but having itching ears they will accumulate for themselves teachers to suit their own passions, and will turn away from listening to the truth and wander off into myths. As for you, always be sober-minded, endure suffering, do the work of an evangelist, fulfill your ministry." — 2 Timothy 4:3-5 (ESV)

How to identify false teachers?

"And when they say to you, "Inquire of the mediums and the necromancers who chirp and mutter", should not a people inquire of their God? Should they inquire of the dead on behalf of the living? To the teaching and to the testimony! If they will not speak according to this word, it is because they have no dawn." — Isaiah 8:19-20 (ESV)

"Beware of false prophets, who come to you in sheep's clothing but inwardly are ravenous wolves. You will recognize them by their fruits. Are grapes gathered from thornbushes, or figs from thistles? So, every healthy tree bears good fruit, but the diseased tree bears bad fruit. A healthy tree cannot bear bad fruit, nor can a diseased tree bear good fruit. Every tree that does not bear good fruit is cut down and thrown into the fire. Thus you will recognize them by their fruits. "Not everyone who says to me, 'Lord, Lord,' will enter the kingdom of heaven, but the one who does the will of my Father who is in heaven. On that day many will say to me, 'Lord, Lord, did we not prophesy in your name, and cast out demons in your name, and do many mighty works in your name?' And then will I declare to them, 'I never knew you; depart from me, you workers of lawlessness.'" — 1 Timothy 6:3-10 (ESV)

"Children, it is the last hour, and as you have heard that antichrist is coming, so now many antichrists have come. Therefore we know that it is the last hour. They went out from us, but they were not of us; for if they had been of us, they would have continued with us. But they went out, that it might become plain that they all are not of us. But you have been anointed by the Holy One, and you all have knowledge. I write to you, not because you do not know the truth, but because you know it, and because no lie is of the truth. Who is the liar but he who denies that Jesus is the Christ? This is the antichrist, he who denies the Father and the Son. No one who denies the Son has the Father. Whoever confesses the Son has the Father also." — 1 John 2:18-23 (ESV)

"But the fruit of the Spirit is love, joy, peace, patience, kindness, goodness, faithfulness, gentleness, self-control; against such things there is no law. And those who belong to Christ Jesus have crucified the flesh with its passions and desires. If we live by the Spirit, let us also keep in step with the Spirit. Let us not become conceited, provoking one another, envying one another." — Galatians 5:22-26 (ESV)

Can we judge and expose false teachers?

"As I urged you when I was going to Macedonia, remain at Ephesus so that you may charge certain persons not to teach any different doctrine, nor to devote themselves to myths and endless genealogies, which promote speculations rather than the stewardship from God that is by faith. The aim of our charge is love that issues from a pure heart and a good conscience and a sincere faith. Certain persons, by swerving from these, have wandered away into vain discussion," — 1 Timothy 1:3-6 (ESV)

"Take no part in the unfruitful works of darkness, but instead expose them." — Ephesians 5:11 (ESV)

"This charge I entrust to you, Timothy, my child, in accordance with the prophecies previously made about you, that by them you may wage the good warfare, holding faith and a good conscience. By rejecting this, some have made shipwreck of their faith, among whom are Hymenaeus and Alexander, whom I have handed over to Satan that they may learn not to blaspheme." — 1 Timothy 1:18-20 (ESV)

Watch out for false doctrine

"I am astonished that you are so quickly deserting him who called you in the grace of Christ and are turning to a different gospel— not that there is another one, but there are some who trouble you and want to distort the gospel of Christ. But even if we or an angel from heaven should preach to you a gospel contrary to the one we preached to you, let him be accursed. As we have said before, so now I say again: If anyone is preaching to you a gospel contrary to the one you received, let him be accursed." — Galatians 1:6-9 (ESV)

"Everyone who goes on ahead and does not abide in the teaching of Christ, does not have God. Whoever abides in the teaching has both the Father and the Son. If anyone comes to you and does not bring this teaching, do not receive him into your house or give him any greeting, for whoever greets him takes part in his wicked works." — 2 John 1:9-11 (ESV)

"I appeal to you, brothers, to watch out for those who cause divisions and create obstacles contrary to the doctrine that you have been taught; avoid them. For such persons do not serve our Lord Christ, but their own appetites, and by smooth talk and flattery they deceive the hearts of the naive." — Romans 16:17-18 (ESV)

"See to it that no one takes you captive by philosophy and empty deceit, according to human tradition, according to the elemental spirits of the world, and not according to Christ. For in him the whole fullness of deity dwells bodily," — Colossians 2:8-9 (ESV)

Warning against adding, taking away, and twisting scripture

"I warn everyone who hears the words of the prophecy of this book: if anyone adds to them, God will add to him the plagues described in this book, and if anyone takes away from the words of the book of this prophecy, God will take away his share in the tree of life and in the holy city, which are described in this book." — Revelation 22:18-19 (ESV)

Testing spirits by guarding yourself with the Bible

"Beloved, do not believe every spirit, but test the spirits to see whether they are from God, for many false prophets have gone out into the world. By this you know the Spirit of God: every spirit that confesses that Jesus Christ has come in the flesh is from God, and every spirit that does not confess Jesus is not from God. This is the spirit of the antichrist, which you heard was coming and now is in the world already. Little children, you are from God and have overcome them, for he who is in you is greater than he who is in the world. They are from the world; therefore they speak from the world, and the world listens to them. We are from God. Whoever knows God listens to us; whoever is not from God does not listen to us. By this we know the Spirit of truth and the spirit of error." — 1 John 4:1-6 (ESV)

"but test everything; hold fast what is good." — 1 Thessalonians 5:21 (ESV)

"All Scripture is breathed out by God and profitable for teaching, for reproof, for correction, and for training in righteousness, that the man of God may be complete, equipped for every good work." — 2 Timothy 3:16-17 (ESV)

We are commanded to rebuke false teachers

"preach the word; be ready in season and out of season; reprove, rebuke, and exhort, with complete patience and teaching." — 2 Timothy 4:2 (ESV)

"But avoid foolish controversies, genealogies, dissensions, and quarrels about the law, for they are unprofitable and worthless. As for a person who stirs up division, after warning him once and then twice, have nothing more to do with him, knowing that such a person is warped and sinful; he is self-condemned." — Titus 3:9-11 (ESV)

Other reminders regarding heresy

"so that we may no longer be children, tossed to and fro by the waves and carried about by every wind of doctrine, by human cunning, by craftiness in deceitful schemes. Rather, speaking the truth in love, we are to grow up in every way into him who is the head, into Christ," — Ephesians 4:14-15 (ESV)

"For certain people have crept in unnoticed who long ago were designated for this condemnation, ungodly people, who pervert the grace of our God into sensuality and deny our only Master and Lord, Jesus Christ." — Jude 1:4 (ESV)

False teachers may look like Christians and do good deeds and mighty works, but even Satan disguises himself

"For such men are false apostles, deceitful workmen, disguising themselves as apostles of Christ. And no wonder, for even Satan disguises himself as an angel of light. So it is no surprise if his servants, also, disguise themselves as servants of righteousness. Their end will correspond to their deeds." — 2 Corinthians 11:13-15 (ESV)

"having the appearance of godliness, but denying its power. Avoid such people." — 2 Timothy 3:5 (ESV)

"You are of your father the devil, and your will is to do your father's desires. He was a murderer from the beginning, and does not stand in the truth, because there is no truth in him. When he lies, he speaks out of his own character, for he is a liar and the father of lies." — John 8:44 (ESV)

ABOUT THE AUTHOR

Richard P. Moore is currently serving with TeachBeyond in Germany in the Theology and Innovation department. He has lived with his family in Germany for over two years. Richard has served as a youth pastor for more than 20 years in various churches. He graduated from Columbia International University (Columbia, South Carolina) in 1998 with a Bachelor of Science in Bible and Youth Ministry. Richard returned later to complete his Master's Degree in Leadership, Evangelism, and Discipleship in 2004 from Columbia International University. Richard is currently pursuing his Doctor of Ministry Degree at American Baptist Seminary of the West in Berkeley, CA (in partnership with Bakke Graduate University in Seattle). He is married to Simone Müller-Moore. They have three children: Ana, Lydia, and Caleb. Richard enjoys sports, adventures with his family, and watching movies and TV shows together with them. Richard is also very active in church development and church planting in Germany. Richard is passionate about seeing an ever-increasing number of young people come to know, worship, and obey Jesus authentically.

Made in the USA
Columbia, SC
30 May 2018